WORLD MAP

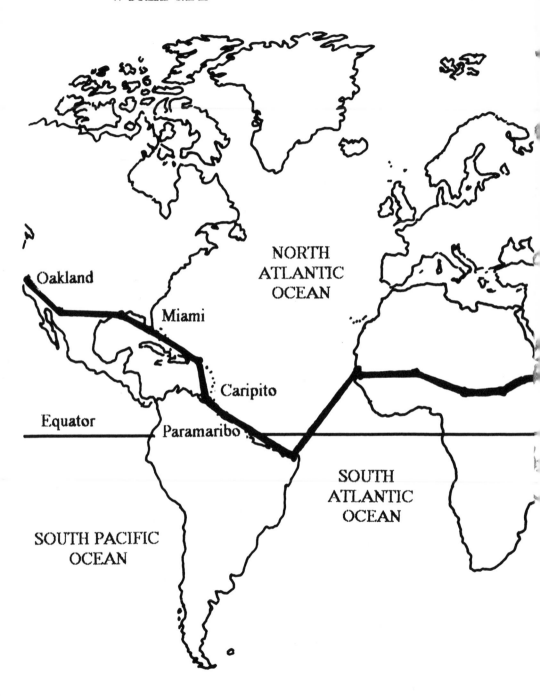

Oakland

Miami

NORTH
ATLANTIC
OCEAN

Caripito

Equator

Paramaribo

SOUTH
ATLANTIC
OCEAN

SOUTH PACIFIC
OCEAN

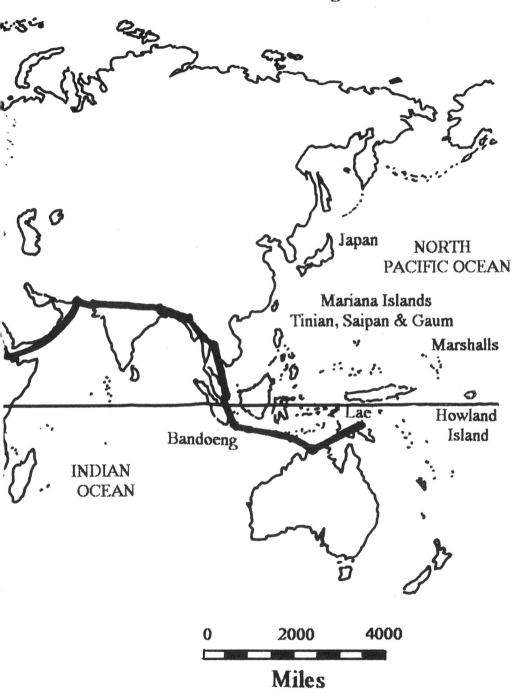

Route of Amelia Earhart's
Round the World Flight in 1937

Japan

NORTH
PACIFIC OCEAN

Mariana Islands
Tinian, Saipan & Gaum

Marshalls

Bandoeng

Lae

Howland
Island

INDIAN
OCEAN

0   2000   4000

Miles

"By carefully comparing the response patterns of witnesses to the Amelia Earhart tragedy, Don Wilson not only enters the circle of scholars on the subject, he has also likely revealed what indeed happened."—Paul A. Miller, Ph.D., LLD, president emeritus, Rochester Institute of Technology.

"Don Wilson's book was so good, so interesting, I couldn't put it down. He has created a superb anthology long-awaited amongst serious Earhart researchers."—Bill Prymak, president, The Amelia Earhart Society of Researchers.

"Don Wilson, having witnessed first-hand the Hindenburg tragedy and western Pacific portions of World War II, has now creatively researched and written what may be the definitive Amelia Earhart tragedy text. The organization of this book and its consistent probing for the real truth make it difficult for the reader to put down, once Don has enrolled him or her in the search."—Ralph H. Stearns, vice president emeritus, Rochester Institute of Technology Research Corporation.

"I have read Don Wilson's book with a critical eye, but find nothing I would change or refute. Thanks to his work, we have a detailed and comprehensive summary of what most probably happened to Earhart and Noonan after their disappearance. I hope his book receives the recognition it deserves."—Paul Rafford., Jr., former radioman with Pan Am and long-time Earhart researcher.

"*Don Wilson's presentation of the information [is] absolutely fascinating. I couldn't put it down until I had finished. He has a winner. With all the witnesses who must have identified Earhart and Noonan in the Marshalls and on Saipan, there must be some truth that they were there. If not, who was it that all these people saw?*"—Colonel Rollin C. Reineck (Ret.) chief navigator for B-29s on Saipan, during World War II.

"*I found Don Wilson's course on Amelia Earhart to be intriguing and thought-provoking. It is a subject I had not thought about in years, and it piqued my curiosity. It was a fair presentation of many diverse theories as to her fate, and made me curious to know more about the resolution of this unsolved mystery.*"— Sally Bludeau, secretary, Athenaeum Council.

"*... the most complete, concise, and chronological reports of those who remember seeing two white persons, most probably Amelia and her navigator, Fred Noonan, after July 2, 1937. With the testimony of so many credible witnesses, it might well be said that the myth of her disappearing in the Pacific Ocean has been effectively dispelled.*"—Ann Holtgren Pellegreno, an author and researcher who flew a Lockheed 10A around the world, following the flight path of Earhart's plane 30 years later.

Amelia Earhart: Lost Legend

To Bill and Vivienne —
    Nice to have you as
good neighbors at Morehouse Lake
    Good reading!

                Best wishes,
        Donald Moyer Wilson

Amelia Earhart: Lost Legend

Accounts by Pacific Island Witnesses of the Crash, Rescue and Imprisonment of America's Most Famous Female Aviator and Her Navigator

Donald Moyer Wilson

Enigma Press

Manufactured in the United States of America

Library of Congress Number: 93-72991

ISBN: 0-9637777-0-X paperback edition
ISBN: 0-9637777-1-8 casebound edition

? ENIGMA PRESS
One Woods Point
Webster, New York, 14580

Dedication

To my wife, Vernajean,
for her encouragement,
patience and love
as we travel through life together.

CONTENTS

Illustrations

Sketches by David Mancini

Maps

by Russell Reynolds

Foreword

WE, WHO WERE KIDS when Amelia Earhart and Fred Noonan were lost somewhere in the then mysterious Pacific archipelago had, in effect, grown up with aviation. Those of us who had lived in small towns or in the country used to hope that the infrequent appearance overhead of a war-surplus "Jenny" signified a forced-landing about to take place in a farmer's field or, even better, a planned landing by a barnstormer who would spend a day or two taking those of us who could afford it up for flights (helmet and goggles supplied) and drawing a crowd by performing "stunts."

All of us, city-kids or country-kids, thought of fliers as the doomed, romantic figures that we met in books about the flying squadrons of the First World War or in movies like *Wings*. Even the emergence of commercial aviation did not make flying mundane. Flying the mail still connoted visions of leather jackets, silk scarves, helmets and goggles, and people who some years later actually went from city to city in Ford Trimotors were glamorous adventurers, not travelers.

It is no wonder that Charles Lindbergh had been a hero adulated beyond any adulation that has been accorded subsequent heroes. His solo transatlantic flight in 1927 was the ultimate achievement in the death-defying exploits of aviators. It may have been only a triumph of a technology unbelievably primitive when compared with a technology that was later to land men on the moon, but we did not of course see it that way. We saw "Lucky Lindy," "The Lone Eagle" as the embodiment of all our fantasies about men in flight.

We continued to be preoccupied with Charles Lindbergh as he moved on to epochal flights emblematic of the rapid strides then being made in aviation. He now shared his adventures with a beautiful and talented wife, whose way with words helped us to see the heroes of the age of flight in poetic terms. But the godlike Lindberghs were cast down to a human level of suffering when their child was kidnapped and killed and they were subjected to unrelenting public scrutiny throughout the capture, trial and execution of the kidnapper, Bruno Richard Hauptmann.

The stage vacated by our god of the air was set for the appearance of a goddess of the air. As aviation was becoming more a part of our everyday lives, aviators were losing their glamour. But not what we called then the "aviatrix." The frontier now to be conquered was mastery of the air by women. When Lindbergh became an expatriate in 1935, I can remember that we were thrilled by the prospect of goddesses of the air taking over the challenge. There were a number of women fliers who performed spectacular feats, but the slim, apparently reticent, amazingly accomplished and courageous Amelia Earhart captured the public imagination in a way that none of her fellows did.

Her disappearance at the height of her career, the mystifying circumstances that accompanied it, and its vague associations with what we were coming to regard as menacing forces in the western Pacific pointed to another stage in our fascination with airplanes and the people who fly them. Long over-water flights were now no longer of compelling interest unless they ended in disaster for famous people as had the Will Rogers and Wiley Post flight in 1935. But to lose Amelia Earhart was to have the gods hurl down one of the best exemplars of "modern woman" before she had time to earn her place in the pantheon of aviation.

That is why I, who have no curiosity about unsubstantiated sensational stories about bizarre events that appear in the tabloids, have so enjoyed reading Donald Moyer Wilson's book, *Amelia Earhart: Lost Legend*. Those of us who are still thrilled to have been part of the age of flight—and who can say he's not?—want to know what happened to the goddess of that age, and we need a guide on that quest.

Don Wilson knows that we could be led down a hundred paths, some fascinating, some not so, but he has surveyed the literature and to some extent the oral tradition to give us an overview of what has been, more than fifty years now, a growing body of speculation about the fate of Amelia Earhart and her navigator, Fred Noonan. Best of all, he has examined the evidence through the eyes of the normally curious reader who has no ax to grind other than to put things in such order that we will be able to have an unobstructed view of various accounts.

His interest is not that of a lawyer who must prove the case beyond a reasonable doubt and not that of the historian who must subject the data to rigorous standards of corroboration and evaluate the reliability of witnesses. His interest is to examine the tradition dispassionately, which he does throughout the book, and he will at the end come up with what seems to him the most likely account of the fate of Earhart and Noonan. However, he will provide for you—as he has for me—the thrill of the chase as we run down the trail to the solution of the mystery. He knows, as you will come to know, that what he has written here is just a stage on the continuum. New speculation and new evidence come in almost daily. Maybe we will conclude that the mystery here—unlike the mysteries in mystery stories—can be solved only tentatively and that—as in life—the joy is in the seeking.

Chester Baum
Chairman, Department of English (Retired)
St. Andrews School, Middletown, Delaware

A veteran of WW II, Lt. Cmdr. (U.S. Naval Reserve) Baum served in the Office of Naval Intelligence, and was on Saipan and Tinian briefly after the hostilities were over.

Preface

*W*HAT REALLY HAPPENED to America's most famous female aviator and her navigator near the equator in the summer of 1937? Did her Lockheed *Electra* run out of gas during their round-the-world flight and crash into the Pacific Ocean? Was it shot down during a spy mission over a secret naval base? Did Amelia Earhart and Fred Noonan survive an emergency landing only to be captured and imprisoned? Which of the stories of those who claim to be eyewitnesses are the most credible, and are the reports of those who talked with those witnesses accurate? Finally, is there a way of fitting together the most probable events into a coherent narrative of what really happened?

What is known is that on July 2, 1937, the world-famous American aviator, Amelia Earhart, and her navigator, Fred Noonan, were nearing the end of their exhausting flight. Over the middle of the Pacific Ocean they were running low on fuel and could not locate the tiny island which was their next destination. Radio communication was poor. Then it ceased completely. There was only silence.

A massive sea and air search conducted by the U.S. Navy for many days failed to produce any significant clues. Amelia's husband, George Putnam, did everything he could to have her found, but his efforts were fruitless.

Eventually the search was terminated. It was assumed that their plane had gone down in the ocean and that they had not survived the crash.

* * *

But did they? Many people have attempted to discover another account of what really happened to Amelia Earhart and her navigator. Some have engaged in years of research, traveled great distances, and interviewed a number of people. Natives from several remote islands in the Pacific have testified that they saw two white foreigners in the summer of 1937 and identified them as American fliers. Most natives said they saw a man and a woman with short hair who was dressed like a man. A few observed that the man's head was injured and that he sometimes needed help to move. The islanders had been told that the fliers were spies. Some were later even able to identify photographs of the woman and recall her name as Amelia Earhart!

As a boy, I remember reading and hearing radio reports about the disappearance of Amelia Earhart and the unsuccessful search. During World War II, I served as a marine on the island of Saipan, located in the Mariana Islands, 1,275 miles south of Tokyo. I later learned that some servicemen had found evidence on Saipan that Amelia Earhart may have been imprisoned there.

In 1991, I decided to return to the places where I had served during and after the war. My chief motive in going to Saipan, was to show the island to my wife, Vernajean. While I was intrigued by the Earhart connection with the island, I had not expected to find myself caught up in the opportunity to gather information from witnesses. Before starting the trip, however, I did read several books on Earhart and talked with the authors of two of the books. Vernajean and I toured the island by ourselves for about a week making some casual inquiries about the possible presence of Earhart on the island. Most people did not think there was much to the story.

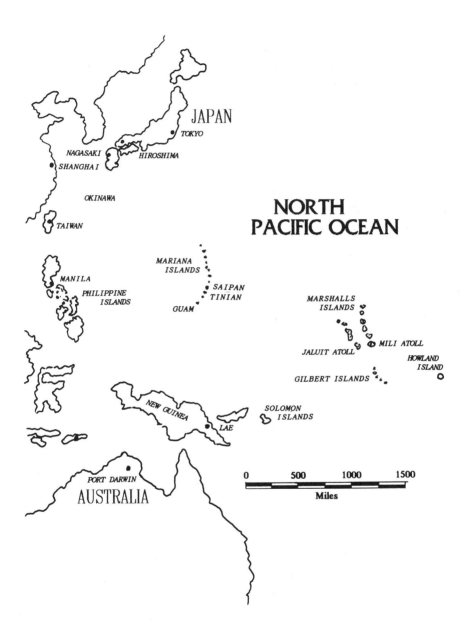

JAPAN

TOKYO

NAGASAKI   HIROSHIMA

SHANGHAI

OKINAWA

TAIWAN

NORTH PACIFIC OCEAN

MARIANA
ISLANDS

MANILA

PHILIPPINE
ISLANDS

SAIPAN
TINIAN

GUAM

MARSHALLS
ISLANDS

JALUIT ATOLL

MILI ATOLL

HOWLAND
ISLAND

GILBERT ISLANDS

NEW GUINEA

SOLOMON
ISLANDS

LAE

PORT DARWIN

AUSTRALIA

| 0 | 500 | 1000 | 1500 |

Miles

It was not until I began talking with a former island senator, Manny Muña, about his personal experiences that I became consumed with the desire to learn all I could about the Earhart-Noonan mystery.

After returning to the United States, I gathered more information about the fliers from books, magazines, newspapers, TV documentaries and personal conversations. I began sharing this information on the Earhart-Noonan mystery in an adult education class. My experiences in this class showed me the need to focus on the cumulative testimony of those who had any knowledge of these two Americans to find clues as to what most probably happened.

This book is an expansion of the work that I have done with my classes. It offers the testimony of a greater number of witnesses than has yet been collected in any single source. I have chosen to examine what seems to be the most credible testimony reported in previous works and by the individuals with whom I have personally spoken and corresponded. The authors repeatedly comment on the apparent sincerity of the witnesses. The Roman Catholics interviewed in the presence of a priest would have little reason for lying. Authors continually questioned the motivation a person had for telling a story—or not telling it. There was no monetary gain for the witnesses, as no money was offered. While the various authors have sometimes used different spellings for the name of the same person, this is to be expected in transcriptions of oral testimony and does not indicate that these were different witnesses. I have chosen what I consider to be the most consistent or accurate spelling for the name of an individual.

The books which I have found particularly helpful and from which I have used considerable material, are:

The Search for Amelia Earhart by Fred Goerner (1966)

Amelia Earhart Returns From Saipan by Joe Davidson, (1969)

Amelia Earhart Lives by Joe Klaas (1970)

Amelia Earhart: Her Last Flight by Oliver Knaggs (1983)

Amelia Earhart: The Final Story by Vincent Loomis and Jeffrey Ethell (1985)

Eyewitness: The Amelia Earhart Incident by Thomas E. Devine with Richard Daly (1987)

Witness to the Execution by T.C. ("Buddy") Brennan (1988)

Over the years in my professional work as a clergyman and as a manager, I have spent considerable time comparing various accounts of the same event in order to determine which version seemed most accurate. I have drawn on this experience for my work with this book.

I am indebted to those who helped me to come up with the title of this book: *Amelia Earhart: Lost Legend,* which I first resisted in favor of others I had selected. But when I continued to think about the meaning of the word, legend, it seemed entirely appropriate. Here is how the dictionary defines it: "Any story coming down from the past, especially one popularly taken as historical though not verifiable; also such stories and traditions collectively, especially of a particular people."[1]

Amelia Earhart is indeed an American legendary figure, who became lost in 1937 with her navigator, Fred Noonan. But there are also numerous stories of their survival which have become legends. I have put them together into a single story that has not been told in this way before—the legend of the lost heroine.

Appearing for the first time in any book will be transcriptions of the recorded conversations which I had with Muña plus information given to me by Bill Prymak, an engineer and president of the Amelia Earhart Society of Researchers. I am also indebted to Paul L. Rafford, Jr., a former radio operator with Pan Am; Albert Bresnik, Amelia Earhart's personal photographer; Colonel (Ret.) Rollin C. Reineck, chief navigator for the B-29s on Saipan during World War II, and Jerome P. Steigmann, a police detective and former marine, who has been an Amelia Earhart researcher since 1944, for the information they have given me. I would like to thank the authors and other Amelia Earhart Society researchers with whom I have spoken and corresponded, for their generosity in sharing opinions and information beyond what they have personally put into print and for allowing me to use the fruits of their labors in this book.

To make this material useful to other Earhart investigators and scholars as well as to the general reader, I have provided statements of eyewitnesses grouped according to subject matter along with notes and an index. Additionally, for basic background information, there is a list of names appearing near the end of the book, with brief identifications of all witnesses, and a list of places.

I hope, that by letting the witnesses speak, we may come closer to the truth of the final days and years of Amelia Earhart and Fred Noonan. And in that spirit, I welcome communication from those who may have information which might be included in future editions of this book. I hope also to write a second book using information I now have and some I hope to obtain dealing with the question of the true nature of the mission of Amelia Earhart and Fred Noonan in their attempted equatorial flight around the world.

Donald Moyer Wilson
Webster, New York, 1993

Acknowledgments

*I*T WOULD BE IMPOSSIBLE to recognize everyone who has helped make this book become a reality. But I would like to give credit to a number of people who have made my work so enjoyable.

Researchers with whom I have corresponded, or with whom I have talked with on the phone or in person: Buddy Brennan; Tom Devine; JoAnn Ridley; Paul L.Rafford, Jr.; Bill Prymak; Rollin C. Reineck; Joe Gervais; Joe Klaas and Jerry Steigmann. Also, Manny Muña on Saipan for his courtesy, enthusiasm, and valuable information.

Staff members of the many Rochester-area libraries who have not only checked out books, but have helped me locate hard-to-find books elsewhere.

The teachers (Carole McAlister and Barbara Murphy) and students of writing classes I attended in Port Charlotte, Florida and Rochester, New York while the book was in preparation.

The staff at Mailboxes, Inc. (Sally Kepplinger, Deborah Kuhs, Mary Ellen Heyman, Steven Taylor and Shellie Levy), where I frequently used and experimented with copy machines while making various drafts of the book.

Pierre's World of Travel, which helped us with our travel plans to Saipan and other places in the Pacific.

The Library of Congress for making a list of books on Amelia Earhart available and for use of some of them. The Smithsonian

Institution and Al Bresnik for photographs of Amelia Earhart.

Russell Reynolds for the maps which he drew and David Mancini for his pen and ink sketches. Nancy Brush and Bob Smith for inviting me to appear on Bob's talk show on WXXI-AM.

Class members at the Rochester Institute of Technology's Athenaeum; attendees at various programs, and friends. They have shown interest and enthusiasm for the material presented, raised perceptive questions, read various drafts of my manuscript, shared clippings and other information they have discovered, called attention to television programs, or have given me help in a variety of ways—and most of all have encouraged me to write this book. I want to thank particularly: Florence Baxter; Gordon Beckwith; Doug Borden; Bob Brennan; Mary Lou Carlson; Grace Collins; Katrina Chubbuck; Joyce Cole; Jim Eagen; Ted Ellstrom; Andrea Frost; Betsy Gibson; Mary Huyck; Clarence La Count; Ann Marks; Paul Miller; Peg Muto; Marjorie Nichols; Sarepta Ostrum; Lemar Plunkett; Helen and Ruth Post; Jim Robertson; Stephen Salai; Kathy Schmidt; Grizel Spence; Jack Stateler; Ralph Stearns; Peg Toker; Suzanne Travers; Carolyn Turner; Bob Vreeland; Bob Wilkin; Katie Williams; Ed Winkler and Stan Zack. The list should be longer, but others who have helped in any way will know who they are.

Finally a big "thank you" to my new friends in Charlotte County, Florida: Chester Baum for his considerable editing and Jim and Linda Salisbury for letting themselves get involved in a much bigger project than they had anticipated!

Amelia Earhart in 1937 as photographed by her personal photographer, Albert L. Bresnik, and used by permission.

Amelia Earhart climbing out of the cockpit of her Lockheed 10E Electra, at Caripito Airport, Caripito, Venezuela, on arrival from San Juan, Puerto Rico, June 2, 1937. (With permission, Smithsonian Institution.)

Two professional photographs of Amelia Earhart taken by her personal photographer, Albert L. Bresnik, and used by permission.

Amelia Earhart receiving the National Geographic Society Medal from President Herbert Hoover in recognition of her non-stop solo flight across the Atlantic, June 21, 1932. L-R: Dr. Grosvernor (society president), President Hoover, Earhart and Mrs. Hoover. (With permission, Smithsonian Institution)

L-R. Paul Mantz, Amelia Earhart, Harry Manning and Fred Noonan in front of Earhart's Electra prior to taking off from Oakland, California for Honolulu, Hawaii, March 18, 1937. (With permission, Smithsonian Institution.)

Paul Mantz, Amelia Earhart and Fred Noonan in Hawaii on first unsuccessful round-the-world flight, circa March 17, 1937. (With permission, Smithsonian Institution.)

Amelia Earhart shown walking with her husband, George Putnam. (With permission, Smithsonian Institution.)

Amelia Earhart in front of Lockheed 10E Electra *and below, seated on horizontal stabilizer of her plane. (Photos used with permission of Smithsonian Institution.)*

Fred Noonan and Amelia Earhart in front of Electra *at Caripito Airport, Caripito, Venezuela, exactly one month before their disappearance. (With permission, Smithsonian Institution.)*

Amelia Earhart standing in front of Electra, *as photographed by her personal photographer, Albert L. Bresnik, and used by permission.*

Introduction:
My Return to Saipan, 1991

"In this cell was Amelia Earhart. These two cells held the cattle rustlers. Cell No.4 held Fred Noonan."—Manny Muña to author, April 9, 1991.

M ARCH 30, 1991. The Tokyo airport was crowded. There were long lines of people everywhere. Vernajean and I wondered how we could possibly board our plane to Saipan in time. We had just completed a two-week tour of Japan and our flight from Osaka arrived later than was originally scheduled. Then we were delayed by red tape as we transferred from one flight to another.

Our final barrier was the security section. The lines were so long we knew it would take at least a half-hour to get beyond the check points. But our plane would depart in a few minutes! We had made our reservations for this flight nearly a year earlier and could not take the chance of missing it. Our tickets were good for that flight only, and I didn't know when there would be another plane with available space headed for Saipan. I pleaded with one of the officials saying that we were in a great hurry, only to be told we would have to wait our turn.

What could we do? I scanned the long lines of travelers and spotted an American couple at the head of one of them.

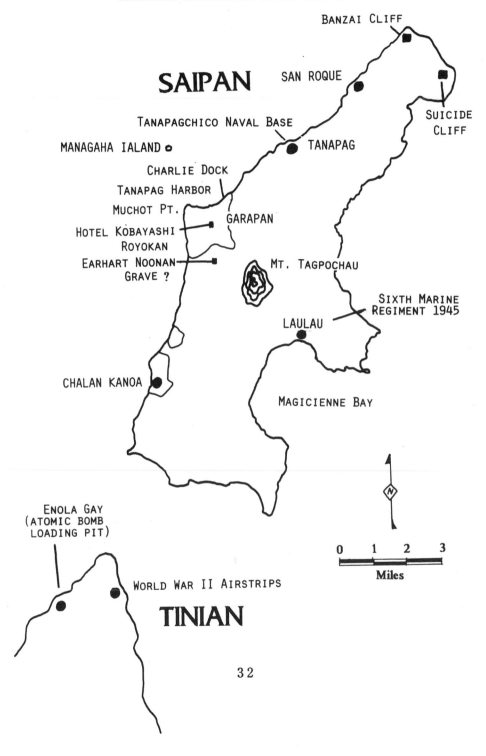

AMELIA EARHART: LOST LEGEND

BANZAI CLIFF

SAIPAN

SAN ROQUE

SUICIDE
CLIFF

TANAPAGCHICO NAVAL BASE

MANAGAHA IALAND

TANAPAG

CHARLIE DOCK

TANAPAG HARBOR

MUCHOT PT.

GARAPAN

HOTEL KOBAYASHI
ROYOKAN

EARHART NOONAN
GRAVE ?

MT. TAGPOCHAU

SIXTH MARINE
REGIMENT 1945

LAULAU

CHALAN KANOA

MAGICIENNE BAY

ENOLA GAY
(ATOMIC BOMB
LOADING PIT)

WORLD WAR II AIRSTRIPS

TINIAN

0   1   2   3
Miles

32

I dashed over, explained my plight and to my great relief, the couple allowed us to get in front of them. Within minutes my wife and I were on the the plane—the last passengers to board. Once in the air, we wondered what to expect upon our arrival on Saipan.

Through the years, Vernajean and I had traveled together to nearly fifty countries. Some we had visited with a group; others we had seen by ourselves. Before each of our trips we would study the travel literature carefully.

Saipan was a different matter. Although the Saipan Tourist Bureau had been helpful, I had been unable to find an American tour which went there, and that was why we were traveling on our own. Surprisingly, most of the famous travel guide books had nothing to say about this island. I located just enough information to make it possible to carry out our plans.

I had spent nearly nine months in 1945 on Saipan as a marine with the Second Marine Division, the final year of World War II. I wanted to see what it was like forty-six years later and to share old memories as well as new experiences with Vernajean.

Two questions went through my mind. Would I be able to recognize the places where I had been on the island? Would I be able to find anything about Amelia Earhart and Fred Noonan by going there?

Like so many other Americans I had been fascinated with the story of Amelia Earhart and her mysterious disappearance in the Pacific.

I remember vividly some of the events of the thirties, because I was born in the previous decade. Living in Plainfield, New Jersey, our family was very much aware of the Lindbergh baby kidnapping and the Hauptmann trial that took place only a few miles away in Flemington. Aviators were perhaps the most celebrated of public figures in those days. Charles Lindbergh had made the first solo flight across the Atlantic in 1927. Amelia Earhart, sometimes called "Lady Lindy," became the first woman to fly a plane across the Atlantic alone. She continued to make daring flights and set new records.

The most terrifying experience of my childhood occurred in 1937 when I was an eleven-year-old school boy. The German dirigible *Hindenburg* had crossed the Atlantic a number of times in 1936, and I remember seeing it pass overhead. The first crossing in 1937 was to bring it in to nearby Lakehurst the afternoon of May 6. My mother drove my sister, me and friends to see it come in to its mooring. The landing was delayed a couple of hours by thunderstorms. Every precaution had to be taken. The dirigible was filled with explosive hydrogen because our government refused to make safer helium available to the Nazis. The excited crowd, including us children, had broken through a rope barrier to run out on the landing field to get a closer look nearer the mooring. At 7:23 P.M. (as I was to learn later), flames started coming out of the airship. At first I thought that this was something that was supposed to happen, but then, as the crowd screamed and ran, I realized a disaster was occurring. The world's largest airship exploded before our eyes. Terrified by the fear that the burning ship might fall on top of us, we turned and ran for our lives.

As witnesses to this tragic event, we were interviewed by the paper the next day, and two days later, we saw the drama depicted in the newsreels before the feature film at the movie theater. The terrifying experience haunted us when we relived the disaster as we watched ourselves on film. Because the explosion and terror are still vivid for me, I think about the witnesses whose testimony I have included in this book–witnesses who include children who were my age at the time of the *Hindenburg* explosion. We as children saw America in the newsreels pulling out of the Depression and we as children came to regard these black and white films as reality.

Through the newsreels we watched armed conflicts in Europe, Africa and Asia. We observed the latest advances in technology. And we learned of Amelia Earhart's latest aviation adventure—a daring flight around the world at the equator.

As spring of 1937 became summer, the newspapers and the radio gave progress reports of this world flight. Earhart had crossed the Atlantic, Africa, southeast Asia. Soon she would fly the Pacific and finish her mission.

Then came the shocking headlines. AMELIA EARHART LOST! Radio contact gone. Out of fuel. Her plane, the *Electra,* must have crashed into the ocean.

But there was hope. Reports came that faint radio signals were being picked up. Maybe she and her navigator, Fred Noonan, were still alive. President Franklin Roosevelt ordered a massive sea and air search for her—the biggest in history. Surely the United States Navy with all of its planes and ships could find her.

The days passed. Hope began to fade. I had assumed the search would continue until they found her. But, unbelievably, they gave it up. They stopped looking for her. Failure. Amelia Earhart, gone. Another major air tragedy in 1937, just a few weeks apart from the *Hindenburg* disaster.

* * *

I do not remember if I heard rumors about Amelia Earhart's imprisonment and death on Saipan during my tour of duty there. I may have. There were all kinds of stories told by servicemen to help relieve the boredom and take our minds off of our own part in the coming invasion of Japan. If I did hear anything, I probably dismissed it as so much "scuttlebutt."

But as the years went by I would occasionally read in *Newsweek* or other publications something about Amelia Earhart and Saipan. Interesting, I thought, I wonder....Then there would be a similar story on television. Hmmm. There would soon be a counter argument to the story and that would seem to be the end of it.

* * *

I do not remember when I first thought about going back to Saipan. It may have been that even when I was in the service it occurred to me that it would be nice to return when I was married and share with my wife the beauty of the island and the water surrounding it. The weather was great. You could see the rain coming, but a few minutes after the rain, the sun would come out and dry you off. We experienced this on our training hikes when we had no place to shelter ourselves. As I prepared for my return to Saipan, I read that the island was listed in the *Guinness Book of World Records* as having the most equable climate in the world. I wasn't surprised.

I could remember the beauty of the stars. They were absolutely dazzling on Saipan in 1945. Every night we would hear from our cots in our tents the haunting strains of Hoagy Carmichael's "Star Dust" played over the area loudspeaker. One night I had guard duty from midnight to 4:00 A.M. The parade of stars across the sky was a marvelous sight. Star dust indeed!

During the days the ocean revealed beautiful shades of blue and green. I had seen nothing like it anywhere before nor have I since.

Would the island be as beautiful as I had remembered? Would the night sky be the same? Had time enhanced my memory of the weather and the ocean? Would Vernajean be let down by reality after my insistence that we visit Saipan? The answers would soon come.

* * *

As we continued on our flight to Saipan, I thought again about Amelia Earhart and what I had read up to that point. While at Cornell University for my fortieth reunion, I had seen in the library a new book about her by Thomas Devine, called *Eyewitness: The Amelia Earhart Incident.* Glancing through it, I saw numerous references to Saipan. Vernajean and I had just returned from the South Pacific and even though I had wanted to visit Saipan on that trip, arrangements seemed too difficult and costly to make at the time. As I looked through the book, I wondered if it might be worth another try.

When we finally decided to go to Saipan a few years later I was not able to locate Devine's book in my local library. So I started reading others. Among them were the following: Fred Goerner's *The Search for Amelia Earhart;* T. C. ("Buddy") Brennan's *Witness to the Execution* and Mary S. Lovell's *The Sound of Wings.*

Brennan had a videotape that was available with his book, so I phoned the publisher for a copy and they had me contact him directly. While ordering the tape I told him of my interest in Amelia Earhart and Saipan. Brennan suggested that upon my arrival I contact a former island senator, Manny Muña, who had been helpful to him.

Brennan's publisher, Renaissance House, had also published Tom Devine's book. When I ordered the book, I asked them to contact Devine for me. That evening he phoned me, and I told him of my interest in Earhart and Saipan. He wondered if I would do a favor for him there. I was happy to help.

* * *

The flight attendant announced we would be landing soon. Through the clouds I could see the island of Saipan. Vernajean was ecstatic about the colors in the water and said she thought she was going to enjoy the island. I had not exaggerated the hues—they were just as I had remembered them.

We landed, stepped out of the plane and onto the ground. The weather was perfect. My memory of the Saipan climate was faultless.

But there were many changes. After all these years, there were no B-29 airplanes on the runway; no jeeps or military trucks on the roads. No soldiers, sailors, or marines anywhere.

Some evidences of World War II remained, however. Block-houses were still standing, converted to civilian use. An American tank remained in the water, a few hundred yards off shore. A huge barge was stranded on a coral reef. Part of a wrecked craft was practically on the beach. "Pillboxes" (rectangular concrete structures that had housed big guns) were evident on shore. In the shallow waters of a neighboring island there was a vehicle with anti-aircraft guns pointed to the sky. There were memorials at Banzai

Cliff and Suicide Cliff where Saipanese civilians had committed suicide rather than be captured by American troops during the invasions of June and July 1944.

In a few days with a rented car I was able to see more of Saipan as a civilian than in the months I had been there as a marine. We drove most of the way up Saipan's highest mountain, Mt. Tagpochou, and climbed the rest of the way. At the top there was a marvelous panaromic view of the island. With my binoculars I tried to make out where the Sixth Marine Regiment and Headquarters Company of the Second Marine Division had been located, since I had been with both. Later we drove to areas that seemed somewhat familiar, but I was frustrated because things looked so different.

I decided not to jump into the Amelia Earhart investigation until I had become more familiar with the island and its people. My casual inquiries of the islanders revealed some familiarity with the stories but not much indication that Earhart and Noonan had ever been on the island.

However, the official tourist map of Saipan did mention Earhart and Noonan and the possibility that they had been there and gave the location of the ruins of the jail, which we located and explored. We even discovered the initials "AE" in one of the cells, but figured this didn't really mean anything as anybody could have put them there.

Vernajean and I were enjoying the excellent facilities of a new hotel. We worshipped in a church one Sunday. After the service I told people I had been on Saipan before. When they asked how things were different now, I replied that the accomodations were much better. The food was great. The swimming was delightful. I went sailing. Vernajean and I played tennis, used the sauna and whirlpool. We enjoyed the fine view of the ocean from the seventh floor of our hotel. Gathering information was not our primary goal.

After a week on the island, I decided to contact Manny Muña. I found his house, but as he was not there, I left a message for him. He called me later, every bit as helpful as Buddy Brennan said he would be, and we got together the next evening at our hotel. Manny is outgoing and we liked each other immediately.

Here is an excerpt of a conversation he permitted me to record:

Muña: "I was born on December 24, 1936, on the island of Saipan. I grew up in a Japanese community. Most of my neighbors were Japanese. We grew up together. That's why I'm able to speak Japanese well.

"I went to school here. We did not have any high school. The highest you could go was ninth grade. When the Catholic mission established a school here, every year they added one grade. The first year it was ninth grade, the next year it was tenth grade, etc. By 1960 that's the time we had non-public school high school.

"So the government also took the initiative of establishing the same path as the Catholic school. It upgraded schools from ninth to twelfth grade. Now we have both Catholic and public high schools. We also have a two-year college here and they are making efforts to have four years of college on Saipan.

"My first college experience was at the University of Hawaii, for two years. Then I attended Syracuse University for two years. I majored in political science. I did not finish the school, because I had to return to Saipan because of the death of my mother. During that time it was very hard to get further education unless you were supported by the government. Scholarships are only for very selected people, you know."

Wilson: "When you came back to Saipan you eventually became a senator?"

Muña: "I was elected first to the House of Representatives. Then I continued all the way up before I changed from the House to the Senate. I became a senator."

Wilson: "What year was that?"

Muña: "I became a senator in 1977. In 1985 I retired."

Wilson: "Now you like to drive a taxi and see the world."

Muña: "I've traveled four times around the world. I've seen a lot of places."

During our visits he gave me an education in the history and political structure of Saipan. And when I mentioned my interest in Amelia Earhart, he began discussing her immediately. Soon Vernajean and I were hearing amazing stories about Amelia Earhart and Fred Noonan from the time of their disappearance to their deaths and Manny offered to take us to see significant sites. Manny is fluent in three languages (Chamorro, Japanese and English.)

Manny asked if we were planning to visit the neighboring island of Tinian, a few miles away. We said we were; we had made reservations to go by boat in two days.

"Why don't you fly there?" asked Manny. "You'll be able to spend more time. You pay my way, and I'll show you all around the island."

"Great!" I said. We cancelled our boat reservations and looked forward to our day with Manny.

The next day I took out my tape recorder and dictated the fascinating information Manny had given to me. It confirmed much of what Buddy Brennan had written in his book. But this was face-to-face contact. This was much more exciting and meaningful. How I wished I had made a greater effort to put the Amelia Earhart-Fred Noonan story together as given by various authors before coming to Saipan. I thought perhaps Manny would let me record what he knew the next time we got together.

* * *

Manny picked us up at the hotel and drove us to the airport. Our flight to Tinian was by a plane that held four people—the pilot and Manny up front and Vernajean and I in back. Within a few minutes we landed at the Tinian airport, where we made arrangements to rent a car for the day.

Manny was an excellent guide. He took us to some ancient ruins on Tinian. We saw a Banzai Cliff on that island also. Then we worked our way over roads which the jungle was beginning to destroy. Our destination was the B-29 runways from which American planes had bombed Japan. Before the end of the war, this complex was the biggest and busiest airport in the world.

While we were sightseeing on Tinian, I asked Manny permission to record what he had to say about Amelia Earhart and Fred Noonan and found he was perfectly willing to have me do so. So I used my camcorder and tape recorder not only to obtain the sights and sounds of Tinian, but also to preserve the story I wanted to know.

We drove to the pits where the atomic bombs had been stored. Each had held one bomb that was later dropped on Japan. Pit No.1 had a sign which told about the bomb used on Hiroshima. Pit No. 2 had a sign which stated that the result of the bomb exploding over Nagasaki was the end of World War II.

These plaques were particularly meaningful to me, as I had been stationed across the water just a few miles away when these planes took off and returned. Because of what they did, I participated in the occupation of, instead of the invasion of, Japan.

Six weeks after the atomic bombs were detonated our marine corps unit went to Nagasaki for three-and-a-half months duty there.

Just a few days before our visit to Saipan, Vernajean and I had visited both Hiroshima and Nagasaki, which are now completely rebuilt. However, the area directly under where the bomb went off over Hiroshima was not rebuilt so that people would be reminded of the horror the Japanese experienced. There was also Peace Park and a museum in Nagasaki. It was a thrill for me to visit the Christian missionary school virtually undamaged by the bomb, for it was here that I had been stationed back in 1945. The outside of the building was just as I had remembered it. The inside had been remodeled but the chapel and auditorium had remained with few changes.

* * *

On Tinian was a plaque showing the streets of the island as they were during the war. Because it is shaped somewhat like Manhattan

Island, Americans had given Tinian's roads names similar to those in the New York City area. The map showed such places as Riverside Drive, Harlem, Central Park, Broadway, 8th Avenue, York Avenue, the Saw Mill River Parkway, 96th Street, 72nd Street, and even the Battery and Chinatown. What an interesting idea—a touch of home for New Yorkers who were thousands of miles away from familiar city streets.

There was also a Seabee memorial, which said: "To the men of the 107th United States Naval Construction Battalion and all the Seabees who in 1944-45 on Tinian, Mariana Islands, participated in the largest engineering feat of World War II. Seabees constructed four runways and created the world's largest airbase enabling the U.S. Armed Forces to end the war in the Pacific. We of the ex-107 CB's consecrate this ground to our fallen comrades. May God help us to avoid World War III. Dedicated November 11, 1985."

There was another memorial to victims of a boat disaster after the war, a reminder that nature exacts its toll on human life as well.

As we were driving around the island, Manny told us not only what he knew about Amelia Earhart and Fred Noonan but also something of the history of Saipan. He even sang this song for us—a song indicating that despite the deaths of heroes and the release of the atomic threat, life goes on.

Upon this hill lies the village of the place I love best.
In my home in Saipan,
Where the roses bloom no more, by a little ranch door,
In my home on the hill of Saipan,
I got a sweetheart waiting there
With dark eyes and curly hair.
Waiting for me back upon the hill.
I'll be happy all my life
If she will be my wife.
I'll be happy in my home in Saipan.
When it's night in my dreams
Take me back where it seems—

Back among the rocks on the hill.
I'll be happy all my life
If she will be my wife.
I'll be happy in my home in Saipan.

* * *

But from their jail cells, Amelia and Fred would not have been able to appreciate the Saipan of this song, if indeed they had been imprisoned there.

After we flew back to Saipan from Tinian, Manny showed us the ruins of the Garapan jail, which Vernajean and I had seen on our own a few days earlier.

"In this cell was Amelia Earhart," he said. "These two cells held the cattle rustlers. Cell No. 4 held Fred Noonan."

Now we knew. Or did we? Did Manny tell of us events that really happened? Or were they just stories?

* * *

Fortunately, there was an unexpected occasion to question him further at the airport, the day we left Saipan to return home. Our flight back to Japan had been cancelled, so we had to wait several hours to take another plane on a different route to Guam, one-hundred-twenty miles away.

While we were waiting, Manny saw us and came over to talk. I had given him my copy of Tom Devine's book, *Eyewitness: The Amelia Earhart Incident.* We started to talk about it. I also asked him for clarification on some of the things that he had told us earlier. Again, I had my recorder with me. What a break for me to have all of this material on tape to review in months to come!

* * *

The task ahead of me was to analyze everything that Manny had said, find all I could about what other writers had discovered, and then come to my own conclusions about the fate of Amelia Earhart, Fred Noonan and their plane.

43

To share my findings, I decided to teach an adult education class for senior citizens on the subject. I could get their reactions and ideas, and encourage them to do their own research. As I put together material for the course, the first stages of this book began to develop.

The enthusiasm and knowledge of the course members was beyond my expectations. One member as a child had had dinner with Amelia Earhart. A second member had a close friend, who was a writer just finishing a book with a chapter containing new information on the famous pilot. A third class member was very helpful in doing research and making useful contacts.

A major amplification of what I had first written, based on comments of my friends, was inevitable. In my first attempt I tried to convince others and myself that Earhart and Noonan may well have survived the crash and lived for a long time afterwards. But the more I went over the material I obtained, and the more I discovered new information, the more certain I became of their survival.

In this book, I have organized witnesses' testimony according to what I consider such crucial questions as: Where did the *Electra* go down and why? Were Earhart and Noonan picked up by the Japanese? Where were they eventually imprisoned? How did they meet their deaths?

Amelia Earhart: Lost Legend will conclude with what I believe really happened to these courageous fliers.

1

First Reports of the Survival

"He tells me that the Japanese have captured an American aviatrix whose plane fell down in the sea between Mili and Jaluit Atoll."–Elieu Jibambam to Oliver Knaggs.[1]

*O*F ALL THE WITNESSES and others who have given reports to investigators about the fate of Amelia Earhart and Fred Noonan, Elieu Jibambam, a Marshall Island native, was perhaps the first person to inform Americans about the crash and their survival. Fred Goerner was the first author to give Jibambam's account in his book, *The Search for Amelia Earhart.*

Goerner, a television news reporter for KCBS in San Francisco came across an article in the May 27, 1960, *San Mateo Times* about a California woman who had lived on Saipan and who had apparently seen Amelia Earhart there. Goerner, at first skeptical, interviewed the woman, Josephine Blanco Akiyama. What she told him was so intriguing that Goerner made four trips to Saipan and one to the Marshalls to learn the entire story.

Fred Goerner's research on the subject of Amelia Earhart and Fred Noonan generated so much publicity that people from all over the United States began contacting him. More and more he realized the possibility that Earhart and Noonan may have gone down in the Marshalls.

Former military personnel who had served during World War II gave him intriguing bits of information.

Fred Goerner

A Berkeley, California real estate man, John Mahan,[2] telephoned Goerner to say that Amelia Earhart crash-landed somewhere between Majuro, Jaluit, and Ailinglapalap in the Marshalls. In 1944, Mahan had been a navy yeoman working with the senior U.S. military government officer, Lt. Eugene Bogan,[3] at Majuro Atoll, after the invasion. They had learned of Amelia's pre-war presence in the area from several English-speaking Marshallese who were serving as interpreters for the military.

Goerner telephoned Bogan, who said that there was no doubt in his mind that Earhart and Noonan had come down in the Marshalls. He had obtained his information about Earhart from a native named Elieu[4] (Jibambam). When Goerner asked Bogan if he believed Jibambam's story, Bogan replied that he had been convinced that it was true from the time he first heard it. He considered Jibambam to be honest and intelligent and did not believe he would have invented such a story. Jibambam had not heard of Amelia Earhart by name before speaking with Bogan. It would seem that an event as important to Americans as the attempted circumnavigation of the globe by a female pilot was probably of little note in the Marshalls. When Goerner visited Jibambam in the Marshalls, he

Elieu Jibambam

found that his testimony was essentially the same as what Bogan had said.

47

Earhart investigator Vincent Loomis had also heard about Jibambam[5] and had talked with him. In 1952 Loomis, an air force pilot, had discovered a wrecked airplane seemingly hidden on a remote atoll in the Marshall Islands. He had wondered at the time if this was the *Electra*—the Earhart plane. A native chief with whom he had spoken seemed to think it was a Japanese plane, but since Loomis and the Americans with him were involved in the H-bomb tests in the area, they did not pursue the matter further.

Years later, however, after reading Paul Briand's *Daughter of the Sky*, Fred Goerner's, *The Search for Amelia Earhart* and other books on the subject, Loomis decided to return. Loomis had discovered that there were many conflicting statements and theories presented by various authors and wanted to check them personally. He retraced his steps in 1978 with his wife Georgie in the Marshalls interviewing as many islanders as possible. On Majuro he was able to interview Elieu Jibambam.

* * *

Oliver Knaggs, another author who has interviewed witnessses, tells his story in *Amelia Earhart: Her Last Flight*, published in South Africa. He had been asked by Vincent Loomis to be with him on his second (1979) expedition to the Marshalls. For some reason, he refers to Loomis only as his leader. It is not always clear to me whether the conversations reported by Knaggs were made in Loomis' presence or with Knaggs alone or whether the people with whom he spoke were contacted more than once.

Knaggs observed that Elieu Jibambam[6] had been asked by the U.S. government to go to Washington to tell officials what he knew about Earhart's capture by the Japanese. Knaggs' conversation with Jibambam was translated by another Marshallese, Dwight Heinie, an administrator.

Another investigator of the Amelia Earhart-Fred Noonan mystery who interviewed Jibambam was a Texas businessman, T.C. ("Buddy") Brennan. Brennan's original intent in visiting the Pacific

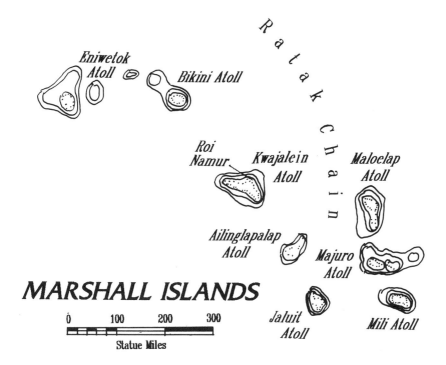

MARSHALL ISLANDS

in the early 1980s, was to search for warplanes from World War II. He planned to take them back to the United States for use in museums, but unfortunately his equipment proved to be inadequate. While he was engaged in his search, he heard stories about islanders, located hundreds of miles apart, who gave similar accounts of two Americans, a man and a woman, who had been captured by the Japanese before World War II.

Brennan made several trips to the Marshalls to try to determine if the people described were Earhart and Noonan, and, using a video camera, interviewed a number of Marshallese. The videotape enables the viewer to observe the witnesses, watch their mannerisms, and listen to their tone of voice. The overwhelming impression I get from watching this tape is of the sincerity of those interviewed.

Brennan says that he was told that an old man who turned out to be Jibambam was willing to talk to the photographers. The Marshall Island native had prepared himself for the interview with a freshly-ironed shirt and trousers but wore the customary thong sandals. Jibambam[7] spoke in English. The interview was held in November, 1983.

* * *

From the reports given to the various investigators, we can reconstruct the following sequence of events:

Elieu Jibambam had worked in 1944 with the senior U.S. military government officer, Lt. Eugene Bogan, at Majuro Atoll helping him apprehend six Japanese. A week or so after Bogan's unit arrived in the Marshalls, Jibambam told his story for the first time. Jibambam had been fearful of telling it until the Marshalls were firmly in American hands. Jibambam asked the Americans if they had heard about the white woman flier who had run out of gas and landed between Jaluit and Ailinglapalap. Since they had not, he told them what he had heard and believed to be true.

A Japanese friend named Ajima had told him about the incident before the war. It was in 1937 when Jibambam was twenty-six years old. Ajima had been a trader with Nanyou Boeki Kaisha, a trading company the Japanese used as a front to cover military activities in the Marshalls and other mandated islands. Jibambam had helped his friend Ajima in the place where he worked. Jibambam said that Ajima had also worked for a Japanese construction company and had gone to many islands to make concrete.

One night Ajima came to Jibambam very excited and asked if he had heard about the two American spies the Japanese had captured. Jibambam said that he had not, although actually other people had told him what had happened. Ajima then whispered the story to Jibambam and insisted that it must be kept a secret. It was too dangerous for Jibambam and Ajima to talk. They spoke in Japanese, as no one was allowed to speak English around the Japanese. Jibambam said that if they had done so they would have

50

had their heads cut off. Jibambam could speak English, but the Japanese did not know this. The Japanese were very secretive and would never talk about what they were doing with their military. It was too dangerous for them and the Marshallese to speak of such things.

Ajima then told Jibambam that the Japanese had captured an American aviatrix whose plane had crashed between Mili and Jaluit Atolls. He mentioned only a woman, although Jibambam thought it was possible there could have been a man in the plane as well. Jibambam commented that the Japanese thought the woman was a spy and that it was very strange that the Americans had used a woman for this purpose. The Japanese were very pleased to capture spies. It was a very big thing for them. Many people there had been killed for being spies. Jibambam had heard about an American marine, Captain Ellis, who, before this incident, had been accused of spying, and was poisoned by the Japanese.

After her crash the woman had been picked up by a fishing boat. Then she was transferred to a ship which carried planes—the *Kamoi* (the *Kamoi* was a 17,000-ton ship that could carry sixteen airplanes)—and was taken to Jaluit, the Japanese headquarters in the Marshalls. Jibambam commented that the Japanese fleet was holding maneuvers in the area at that time. During one of the interviews, Dwight Heinie, acting as interpreter, suggested that if the woman pilot was flying where the fleet was she could have been shot down.

After Jaluit she was taken to Kwajalein—the area naval headquarters for the Japanese. Eventually the woman was taken to Saipan, headquarters for the Japanese in the Pacific.

* * *

It should be emphasized that Jibambam was not an eyewitness. While the Japanese authorities routinely withheld information from the native population, it is not unreasonable to think that his Japanese friend Ajima might have confided in Jibambam, as long as Jibambam would be willing to keep the secret. The importance of

51

Jibambam's testimony is not only that it was first heard in 1944, but also in the sixties, seventies and eighties, and is essentially consistent through those years. Discrepancies occur, but are to be expected in testimony given over a period of forty years. Elieu Jibambam's remarks serve as a good introduction to the testimony of those witnesses who claim to have had a close look at Amelia Earhart and Fred Noonan after the crash.

2

Japanese Pickup at Mili Atoll

"We were told to hurry because they had to go and pick up an airplane and some Americans in Mili."–Tomaki Mayazo to Oliver Knaggs.[1]

A NOTHER WITNESS IN the Earhart mystery is Tomaki Mayazo, who was a teen-aged coal stevedore for the Japanese when the *Electra* went down. Author Vincent Loomis interviewed Mayazo[2] on the Marshall island of Majuro in 1981. Loomis said that Mayazo was friendly but not anxious to tell his story. It was as if he was not sure it should be told to strangers. Other islanders had told Loomis that Mayazo's story was significant, so Loomis persisted until he got a more complete account.

Oliver Knaggs also interviewed Mayazo.[3] He states that after interviewing another islander, Bilimon Amaran, he went into the workshop where Mayazo worked, on the chance that he would be able to talk with him. Mayazo was sitting at his desk, and smiled when he saw Knaggs, who states that Mayazo was an old man now who had recently suffered a stroke, making his speech slurred and difficult to follow.

Brennan's book opens with a conversation with Mayazo,[4] whom he describes as a native inhabitant of the little Marshall island of Majuro. His business was operating a heavy equipment yard. Brennan observed that he was intelligent and articulate, although

53

his speech was slightly blurred from a mild stroke. Their dialogue appears both in Brennan's book and on his videotape. The interview closely resembles the ones Loomis and Knaggs had with Mayazo several years earlier.

* * *

The sequence of events, based on the various accounts, seems to be as follows:

Before the war Tomaki Mayazo had been called out late one night with the rest of his shift to load coal on a Japanese ship—the *Koshu*. (Oliver Knaggs and Bill Prymak assume it is the *Kamoi*, based on testimony they received.) The ship was anchored at Jaluit, the Japanese military and commercial center of the Marshalls in the thirties. The stevedores had to travel out to the ship on a small coal barge.

Mayazo stated that the crew of the ship was quite excited, because they were on their way to pick up some Americans who had crash-landed their airplane in the Marshalls seven to ten days earlier. They were told to hurry. There had been a report on the radio that an American airplane had crashed in Mili. Mayazo said they had to work like machines and that it was very hard. Then an officer came up to them and told them to stop refueling. The ship left very quickly, was gone about a week, and then returned to Jaluit.

The story among the Marshallese was that the captured Americans were then taken to the Japanese base on Roi Namor on Kwajalein in the Marshalls.

In the May 1991 issue of the newsletter published by the Amelia Earhart Society of Researchers, an article written by Bill Prymak and Joe Gervais reports an up-to-date account. On a trip they had recently made to the island of Jabor on Jaluit Atoll, they visited with a soft-spoken elderly gentleman, known as Mr. Hatfield. In broken English, he told them he was once the Mobil agent for the island and had run a small store. Hatfield knew Mayazo as the coal tender who loaded the *Kamoi* and remembered that the ship had left port in a hurry for Mili. It returned a few days later to Jabor under great security.

54

3

Out of Gas, or Shot Down?

"They said her plane was shot down between Jaluit and Mili. One Japanese ship found her and they pick her up and they took her to Mili Atoll. "–Lotan Jack to Buddy Brennan.[1]

"I'm not certain I hit it, but the plane went down and crash- landed just off one of the atolls. The plane I had forced down was flown by a woman. Her name was Amelia Earhart. "–A Japanese pilot to Manuel D. Muña, who told Buddy Brennan.[2]

Lotan Jack

AMELIA EARHART investigator Buddy Brennan learned that Japanese civilians and armed forces stationed in the islands knew of and did talk about the Earhart affair—among themselves at least. Lotan Jack,[3] a Marshallese who had been a coffee maker, or mess steward, for Japanese officers at their headquarters on Jaluit told Brennan that the Japanese had talked of little else for days.

The story Brennan heard was that Lotan Jack was working at the Japanese naval base on the island of Emidj, a part of Jaluit Atoll. Jack learned the story of Amelia Earhart from an officer in the Japanese Navy who said that Earhart's plane was shot down between Jaluit and Mili, about thirty miles from Mili. A Japanese ship found

Lotan Jack

her, picked her up and took her to Mili Atoll. The ship then went to Jaluit and Kwajalein. Her final destination was Saipan.

Jack remarked that the Japanese officer told all the Marshallese not to talk about her, because it was a matter of secrecy. He explained that she had been on a flight around the world and that she was spying at that time for the American people.

Manny Muña

A Marshallese, Dwight Heinie,[4] had spoken earlier to Knaggs of the possibility of the Earhart plane's being shot down, but Knaggs did not investigate this matter further. Brennan might not have given this further thought either until he heard the account given by Manny Muña.[5]

56

When Brennan went to Saipan, he met Muña, a retired senator, who told Brennan the following story, which I also recorded during my trip.

When Muña was a ship's pilot, he had guided ships, using a launch, through a difficult entrance to Saipan's Tanapag Harbor. On one occasion he was assigned to pilot a Japanese ship, the *Fukuun Maru*. As they carefully took the ship into the channel, a twin-engine Beechcraft with easily identifiable twin rudders, flew overhead. The ship's captain casually remarked that the airplane looked like the spy plane that he had shot down a number of years before. He was now about seventy, and the incident he remembered had taken place in 1937.

The captain had gone on to say that he, as a young flight lieutenant aboard the aircraft carrier, *Akagi,* on a training cruise near the Marshalls, had been called to battle stations with the rest of the crew and told that an American spy plane was attempting to photograph Japanese installations. On the subsequent search mission, he saw an airplane which looked almost identical to the twin-engine Beechcraft. He reported this to the commander on board the *Akagi.* To his surprise he was told to force the plane down; to fire on it if necessary.

The American pilot ignored the Japanese pilot as he flew by, so he made a second run as a firing pass. He was not certain he hit it, but the plane went down and crash-landed just off one of the atolls. The pilot returned to the ship, not knowing who had been in the American plane. Later, an officer in Japanese intelligence confided to him that the plane he had forced down was flown by a woman, and that there was also a man aboard. The pilot's name was Amelia Earhart and she was supposed to have been on a flight around the world. The former Japanese pilot had never been able to learn more about the incident.

Brennan's team of researchers on Saipan learned from the shipping company's master file that the pilot's name was Fujie

Firmosa and that he was no longer living. Unfortunately, they were unable to obtain any further information.

At the time of his encounter with Firmosa, Muña had no interest in Amelia Earhart or her fate. But, as a result of this and a later experience, he has done considerable reading about her. As I talked with him, however, I found it difficult to distinguish information which he may have obtained from the pilot from theories which other authors had created.

Kubang Bunitak and Mr. Hatfield

Other reports that a Japanese aircraft carrier pilot may have shot down the *Electra* were obtained recently by Bill Prymak, current president of the Amelia Earhart Society of Researchers. In the May 1991 issue of the society's newsletter there are accounts which add credence to the one given by Manny Muña.

Prymak and Joe Gervais, an experienced researcher, interviewed a doughnut baker, Kubang Bunitak,[6] age seventy-five, who had been at Jabor, the town by Jaluit Harbor on Jaluit Atoll, since 1935. Bunitak told the Society investigators that two American fliers who had been shot down near Mili Island had been brought to Jabor for medical treatment and interrogation.

Prymak writes that he and Gervais learned of a Mr. Lee,[7] to whom a Japanese pilot had told a story that he had shot down Amelia Earhart's plane near Mili Atoll. Prymak and Gervais asked a Mr. Hatfield[8] what he knew about Mr. Lee (Lee had died in 1987). Hatfield told them that Lee had been the chief translator between the Marshallese and the Japanese military. He had been highly respected by Japanese officers and even fraternized with them frequently. On several occasions, Lee had told Hatfield that on July 2, 1937, he (Lee) was out drinking with some high-ranking Japanese naval officers, when one of them suddenly jumped out of his chair, slammed his fist on the table, and boasted to Lee that they knew that the American lady pilot was flying over their islands that night! Lee had also told Hatfield about the arrival of a huge aircraft carrier and war games which were conducted in 1937 at Jaluit and in the surrounding waters.

However, for Prymak and Gervais, the most dramatic moment in the interview occured when Hatfield said that Lee had told him of meeting a carrier pilot who claimed to have shot down Amelia near Mili Atoll.

Gervais had learned from his research many years before that there had been three naval destroyers and one airplane carrier stationed in Jaluit harbor at the time of Amelia Earhart's flight. A captain of a Norwegian ship, Alfred Parker,[9] had seen these ships there and reported them to the United States consul in Japan, Richard F. Boyce.

* * *

Could a Japanese pilot who had served on an aircraft carrier which eventually led the attack on Pearl Harbor and less than a year later was sunk at Midway have survived the war? Most, but not all, Japanese pilots were killed during the war, but the man who led the attack on Pearl Harbor, Captain Mitsuo Fuchida, lived until long after the war was over. I learned this when I had the opportunity of attending a conference in 1958, where Captain Fuchida's son was present. It is, therefore, believable that the man who spoke with Muña about shooting down the *Electra* was an aircraft carrier pilot in 1937.

4

Witnesses to the Crash and Capture

"I saw this airplane and the woman pilot and the Japanese taking the woman and the man with her away."–A boat navigator's wife to Vincent Loomis.[1]

VINCENT LOOMIS WAS the first American to interview Marshall Islanders about the crash of the *Electra*. Oliver Knaggs and Buddy Brennan conducted more interviews. Each author made several trips to the Marshalls.

The Queen of Mili

Each of the researchers talked with the queen of Mili Atoll, Bosket Diklan. She had been married to Takinami, the Japanese commanding officer, who had been the South Seas Trading Company representative on Mili before the war. There is conflicting information from the interviews given to the researchers. It appears that the most accurate and complete information came from the interview with Knaggs. When Knaggs visited the queen,[2] she said she heard that a lady pilot had landed on Mili, although the queen was on another atoll with her husband at the time. Her husband, who had been called to Jaluit, was ordered to return to Japan immediately, without his wife. The queen did not go back to Mili for several months and she never heard from her husband again.

60

Bosket Diklan: Queen of Mili

Knaggs asked who had told her about the crash of the female pilot. She replied that a Marshallese named Lijon[3] had told her after she returned from Mili that he had seen the silver plane landing next to the island of Barre. He had watched while a man and a woman from the plane buried something. Then the Japanese soldiers came to take them away. The queen said she had heard the woman was a spy who was taken to Saipan.

Knaggs asked her if Lijon had gone back to see what the man and woman had buried or to look at the plane. She said he had not, and the Japanese had taken the plane away along with the Americans. There were no Marshallese living on Barre in those days, because the Japanese occupied it.

61

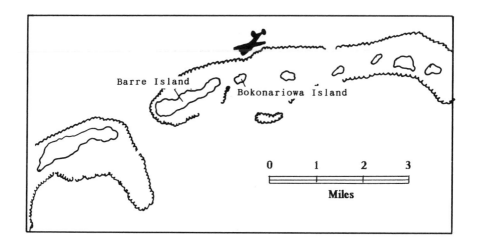

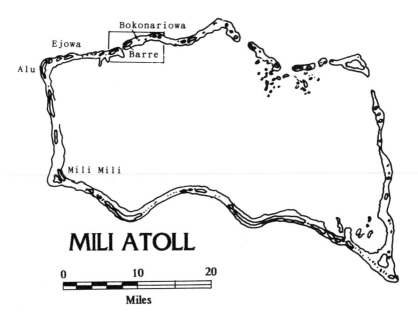

MILI ATOLL

62

The Boat Navigator's Wife

Vincent Loomis talked briefly with a woman who claimed she saw the airplane and a man and a woman who had come from it. She was the wife of the navigator named Clement,[4] who had guided the Loomis party through the waters of Mili Atoll. As Loomis talked with both Clement and his wife, Clement interrupted the questioning and refused to let his wife answer. Although he had not been an eyewitness of Amelia's landing, he silenced his wife every time she tried to speak and answered the questions himself.

Fortunately, Loomis later was able to talk alone with Clement's wife, who insisted that Clement knew nothing. She said she saw the airplane, and the Japanese taking the woman pilot and the man with her away from the atoll. Loomis wanted to know where she had seen the plane. She pointed in the direction of the crash and declared that it was next to Barre Island.

Dr. John

Loomis also talked with Dr. John,[5] a retired businessman who had practiced medicine. Knaggs, who also saw Dr. John,[6] gives the more detailed report.

Knaggs states that he talked with Dr. John at his clinic and learned that he had not come to Mili until 1941. He was originally from the British-ruled Gilbert Islands, south of the Marshalls. Dr. John had been fishing with some friends when they were caught by a storm and blown miles from their home. The Japanese had captured them near Mili.

Eventually Dr. John heard the story that Amelia Earhart had crash-landed on Mili. She and the man with her had been taken prisoner by the Japanese and later sent to Saipan. Dr. John told Knaggs that several years after the end of the war he was shown the prison on Saipan where she had been held captive.

Knaggs comments that it was interesting to learn that someone on Saipan had shown this to Dr. John long before the Americans became involved in investigating her case. In other words, Knaggs believes that the islanders were well aware of Amelia as a prisoner on Saipan, even though American investigators had not yet come to question the islanders about her possible presence on that island.

Lorok

On his second trip to the Marshalls, in the early 1980s, Oliver Knaggs interviewed more islanders. On Mili he met a man named Lorok,[7] who owned Barre Island, a part of Mili Atoll. This was the island near which the crash was said to have occurred.

Lorok said the only person who had actually witnessed the plane coming down was Lijon, who was no longer living. Lorok gave Knaggs an account of Lijon's version of the crash and capture. Lorok was perhaps eleven years old when Lijon told him the news. Lorok said that he had been told later that the people who crashed were Americans. They said little about the man other than that he was hurt. The woman was the focus of their interest, and they said that she was the pilot.

Lorok told Knaggs that he had learned this from the Marshallese people, who in turn had heard it from the Japanese. Lijon told him and others later that the Japanese had taken her to Saipan and killed her as a spy. Nobody at that time was allowed on Mili, as the Japanese were making ready for war, said Lorok. They didn't want anyone to see the fortifications.

Lorok insisted that he thought Lijon was telling the truth. He said the story was confirmed by the Japanese and by other Marshallese, including Bilimon Amaran.

Jororo Alibar

Vincent Loomis interviewed Jororo Alibar,[8] a fisherman, on the island of Ejowa, Mili Atoll. Loomis found him to be pro-Japanese and unfriendly to Americans.

Alibar asked Loomis if he had come to ask about the lady pilot, but was not forthcoming with information until Loomis told him what he had already learned from an American, Ralph Middle, a member of the war reparations group that had come to the islands to assess damage caused by the Japanese. What Middle had told Loomis was that he had learned the story of the two fliers from two Mili fishermen, Jororo Alibar and his friend Lijon. After hearing this, Alibar admitted to Loomis that he knew about the lady pilot and the plane crash. When Loomis then asked Alibar if he knew where the plane went down, Alibar pointed out the reef adjacent to Barre and Bokonariowa islands, in the northern part of Mili Atoll.

Loomis and his group then headed for Barre Island. There he talked with islanders who knew of the crash-landing and insisted that the aircraft had come down near Barre. Some even said that they had seen it shot down in the distance. Loomis remarks that there was no way to prove they had not confused this with something they had seen during World War II.

Lijon's Story

Lijon's story, based on what he had told Middle and Lorok, was this: Some time before the war Lijon was out fishing in the lagoon near Barre. He saw a big silver plane coming. It was low down and he could tell it was in trouble because it made no noise. Then it landed on the reef about two hundred feet from the small island.

He pulled in his fishing line and went quickly to the island to see if he could help. When he got there, he saw strange, unfamiliar people.

He was frightened and hid in the jungle. He watched what he thought were two men get out of the plane into a yellow boat and come ashore. Soon after the two got on the island Lijon saw them bury a silver container in the coral sand under a kanal tree. He could tell that one was hurt because he was limping and there was blood on his face. The other was helping him.

Soon the Japanese arrived and started to question the two fliers. Lijon saw that one was taller than the other. While the fliers were interrogated, the Japanese began to slap them. One started to scream. At that point Lijon realized that this flier was a woman. He remained in hiding because he feared the Japanese would have killed him for what he had seen.

The Search for the Metal Box

Loomis and a Marshall Islander, Gideon Dominic,[9] tried to locate the kanal tree (Barre Island was full of them) under which the container was buried, but even though they used metal detectors, they failed to find the box. Later, Lijon's grandson, Mejin,[10] met Loomis at the Mili airstrip and told the investigative party that they had searched the wrong island for the container; they should have been looking two islands away.

Loomis could not make the search personally at that time. But Oliver Knaggs later returned to Mili and using a good metal detector, searched the two islands near Barre Island with Dominic[11] and others. At the base of a very old kanal tree he found the rusted remnants of a tin container,[12] including a hinge.

Loomis concludes that whatever had been inside had become a solid mass of sand and other materials. He asks how it would have come to rest at the base of a kanal tree under twenty inches of coral sand, unless it had been buried there. He was certain that Fred Noonan's small container had been found just where Lijon had seen it buried.

Knaggs gives a detailed report of his discovery and the difficulties he had finding the metal piece. Upon discovering it, he could not believe it was the metal canister supposedly buried by the Americans back in 1937. He writes that in retrospect he could kick himself for not being more sensible about the find. But he did place the hinge in a little bag to take home where it was analyzed by the metallurgical department of the University of Cape Town, South Africa. The technical report given in Knaggs' book allows him to conclude that, according to the analysis, the hinge could have come from something like a cash box, and could have been part of the canister which Lijon had seen being buried by the fliers.

5

First Aid at Jaluit

"The Japanese...were surprised...that a man with a woman piloting the plane have crashed.... The doctor examined them...and told me to...treat the man; he had a...small cut on the front of his face and his knee....I put some tape on the wounds....I saw the lady, and heard the Japanese call, 'Amira, Amira.' So whether it is Amelia Earhart or not...but I think it she is. It was 1937."—Bilimon Amaran to Buddy Brennan.[1]

ALTHOUGH THERE ARE several witnesses who reported seeing the crash of an American plane in mid-1937, and a number who told of hearing the story, very few have actually reported seeing the man and woman presumed to be Earhart and Noonan. However, one of those who apparently saw the fliers is a man known for his great integrity. Bilimon Amaran's story of how he assisted a doctor who examined the injured Fred Noonan is well-known to the Marshallese. He has been interviewed by several Amelia Earhart investigators, including Brennan, who recorded Amaran's testimony on video-tape.

Amaran's testimony is in fact the strongest of that of any witness in the Marshall Islands that Earhart and Noonan survived their crash. If what he says is true, he saw both of them aboard a Japanese ship, and, as a sixteen-year-old medic, treated the injuries that Fred Noonan received when the plane hit the water.

Loomis identifies Amaran[2] as a Japanese-born store owner living on the island of Majuro. Amaran had been a medical corpsman with the Japanese Navy before and during World War II. He was known as a very religious man and, unlike other Japanese on the island, had treated the Marshallese kindly. He came to love the islands, and after the war, he had settled permanently on Majuro.

Islanders told Loomis that Amaran had had contact with the lady pilot and her male companion. Amaran told Loomis he had no desire to tell stories for personal gain, but Loomis convinced him that he only wanted to talk about what Amaran had seen of the American aircraft and its crew in order to try to solve the mystery of their disappearance.

Amaran's testimony was recorded for Loomis by Jim Slade, who, at that time, was a commentator from radio station WMAL in Washington, D.C.

Oliver Knaggs also interviewed Bilimon Amaran[3] and obtained additional information. Knaggs states that Amaran was sturdily built and well into his sixties. He owned and operated one of the largest stores on the island and was also connected with various other enterprises.

Amaran was also interviewed by Brennan,[4] who describes him as a respected Japanese businessman but who reports that Amaran had been born in the Marshalls, rather than in Japan. Brennan was certain that although he looked only about fifty, Amaran must have been nearly seventy-years old.

Bill Prymak,[5] in an undated newsletter of the Amelia Earhart Society of Researchers, reports the most recent interview with Bilimon Amaran was given to Gervais, Prymak and Bill's son, John, during their trip in 1989. Amaran's testimony was very much like that given to other investigators, although there were some new details. Prymak states that the other investigators, without exception, had found Amaran "unquestionably honest, truthful, and beyond reproach. His story has never wavered, and my two hours with him convinced me beyond any doubt of his total honesty and integrity."

There were also other Marshallese who had known Amaran when he had attended the wounds of the American and who gave substantially similar accounts of the Earhart-Noonan incident.

One such person was Kabua Kabua,[6] whom Knaggs describes as probably the most revered man in the islands, a direct descendent of Kabua the Great,[7] the first king of the Marshalls. This made Kabua Kabua the chief *iroij* (king), which made people respect him even more than the president. At the time Kabua Kabua was the chief of the judiciary in the Marshall Islands.

Knaggs asked Kabua if he remembered the incident about the forced landing of Amelia Earhart, since he had been stationed in Jaluit in 1937. He had been a magistrate on Jaluit, where there were about four or five thousand people at that time. Japanese military people also had been there.

Kabua replied that he remembered a little story about her. Her plane had run out of gas and she had gone down in the area of Mili Atoll. According to the story, a Japanese fishing boat had picked her up and had taken her to Palau or Saipan.

Kabua had talked with Bilimon Amaran who said that he had given medication to the man who was with the lady pilot on the boat at Jaluit. Kabua thought the Japanese regarded her as a spy because Mili was then a big military base. Kabua stated that a Japanese friend of his said that the lady pilot had been attempting a flight around the world. Also, according to the Japanese, the man's head and knee had been injured in the crash.

Bilimon Amaran's Story

Amaran's story, as compiled from the reports of the interviewers, is as follows: Late one night in July, 1937 when he was a sixteen-year-old medical corpsman or trainee in the Japanese navy dispensary (or naval hospital) on Jaluit, he had been called to go on one of the Japanese military cargo ships to attend a wounded person on board. This was a normal duty as the Japanese often called upon him to give medical assistance to the Marshallese. He believed the ship to be the *Kamoi*, as he learned later that the *Kamoi* called at Jaluit during those times, but he could not say for certain it was.

Billimon Amaran

He went to the ship in the middle of the morning with the military director of health services (the chief naval doctor). The crew of the launch that took them to the ship was not allowed to go aboard with them because of the secret nature of what was taking place.

Upon boarding he saw that the crew and officers were in naval uniforms. A woman was sitting in a deck chair and a thin man with wounds was sitting on a hatch cover. They both looked very tired but in good health. He was frightened to discover that his patient was a strange white man—very different from any person he had seen before. These were Americans—until then he only had contact with Marshallese and Japanese people. It did not appear that they were being held as prisoners. He was so nervous that he was almost incapable of attending to the man's wounds. Amaran observed that the man was wounded on the forehead and leg.

The patient had dark hair, blue eyes and a thin mustache. Amaran recalled that the man was a little taller and thinner than himself and remembered the eyes in particular, as they were a very different color from the eyes of the Marshallese.

Loomis tried for several years to find out what color Fred Noonan's eyes were. Finally, a former Pan Am Clipper crewman, Paul L. Rafford, Jr., (who found out from Captain Marius Lodeesen, who had also served with Pan Am), told him that Fred Noonan's eyes were what he called "penetrating blue-gray."

The doctor examined them and said there were no serious injuries and told Amaran to go ahead and treat the man, which he did as best he could. But he was afraid to talk to him or even look at him. The wound on the forehead was minor—there was a slight cut over one eye—but there was a deep infected cut over one knee about four inches wide. It was inflamed and slightly bleeding while Amaran was treating the man. Amaran explained to Loomis that in this tropical climate an open wound can become infected very quickly. He did not stitch the wounds because they were infected, and they had been open for a couple of days. He used what he called "paraply" on the knee. The head wound, which he cleaned, required only a bandage.

Because he spoke only Japanese, he did not talk to either the man or the woman. The man said a few words, but Amaran did not understand him when he spoke to him directly. A Japanese lieutenant on the ship who was fluent in English had served as interpreter.

Amaran described the woman as appearing to be in good health and not needing treatment. She was between five and six feet tall. Her hair was of light color and came down to just below her ears. She looked nice and had a good complexion. He thought she was about thirty-eight. (Earhart was thirty-nine.) He did not know who the woman was, but he did hear her name. The Japanese crew called her, "Amira, Amira." It wasn't until later that he heard the full name of Amelia Earhart so he presumed that this woman was probably her.

Members of the ship's crew told Amaran that the man and woman had been found between the Gilbert Islands and Mili Island of the Marshalls, south of Majuro. He also heard the Japanese officers talk about how the two fliers had been discovered. Their ship had left Mili Island about four or five in the evening. On their way to Jaluit they saw the plane about five or six miles west of Mili Atoll. So they stopped, picked up the two downed fliers, and continued on their trip to Jaluit. The Japanese told him the two were Americans and that their airplane had run out of fuel and come down at Mili. The man had hurt himself when the plane landed. Amaran said that the Japanese seemed to be aware of her flight around the world. A Japanese officer told him that the Americans had flown their airplane from Lae, New Guinea. They tried to reach Howland Island but got lost when they flew into a big storm. They tried to make the Gilbert Islands but were blown off course. They landed in the water next to Mili.

A Japanese officer then took Amaran to the stern of the ship and showed him their airplane. It was silver with two motors and with the left wing broken. The airplane on the back of the ship was still in the canvas slings that had taken it out of the water. Amaran knew Japanese airplanes, but this airplane was unfamiliar to him. It was not Japanese. The airplane was very shiny, like silver. The propellers had only two blades. For the size of the ship it was big, but it did not seem very large for him compared to the size of modern aircraft. Amaran thought he remembered that the Japanese had said the airplane had been taken out of the water, rather than from a coral reef or an atoll. He could not remember if it had numbers on it or not.

It took just a few minutes to treat the two people and he left the ship about an hour after he had come aboard. The doctor stayed to talk with some of the ship's officers. Amaran didn't really know where Earhart and Noonan were taken after he had finished treating the man. He understood the Japanese talking nearby to say the ship was going to leave Jaluit to go to Kwajalein. He remembered that, because he had relatives on Kwajalein. From there it would go to Truk and maybe to Saipan, and if they could make it, to Japan.

Amaran observed that the crew was in total awe that a woman would fly an airplane; this was unheard of in Japan. The talk of the island for a long time was that the plane ended up in Saipan.

According to the rumors he heard, the Americans were taken to Saipan, where they were tried, and found guilty of spying. The man was beheaded, but the woman was put in jail and starved. She died a few weeks later.

6

Interrogation at Jaluit

"In 1937 my father informed us that an American lady pilot had been captured and had been taken to the Japanese high command office in Jaluit."–Oscar (Tony) de Brum to Buddy Brennan.[1]

T WO MARSHALLESE OFFICIALS were interviewed at different times by three of the Earhart investigators—Loomis, Knaggs, and Brennan. One was Senator Amata Kabua, chairman of the Marshall Islands Political Status Commission, which was seeking to restore the islands' independence from the United States. He was soon to become president of the newly-formed Republic of the Marshall Islands. The other was Oscar (Tony) de Brum, vice chairman of the commission, who became the Republic's foreign secretary.

Amata Kabua

Kabua told Loomis[2] only that he believed Earhart had come down in the islands and that her aircraft was still there. This testimony foreshadows reports that run throughout the accounts of the *Electra's* fate.

Tony de Brum

De Brum told Loomis[3] that everyone knew about the woman who was reported to have come down on Mili southeast of Majuro, and who was captured by the Japanese and taken off to Jaluit. He believed this is exactly what happened. He commented that the stories were being told long before Americans began asking questions.

Knaggs told de Brum[4] that Loomis had complained that some of the old Marshallese could tell them a lot but were cautious and holding back. De Brum responded by saying that in 1937 war preparations were already in progress. People did not want to talk about matters which didn't concern them because they could lose their lives. The older people had this so deeply instilled in them that they still felt their lives were in danger and wanted to keep quiet about what happened years before.

De Brum also told Knaggs that the stories about Earhart and Noonan were that they had come down on Mili, were captured by the Japanese and were taken to Jaluit. But he added people said Noonan was hurt in the crash and was treated by one of their Marshallese doctors. Noonan and Earhart were then taken off to Saipan, where Noonan was beheaded. Amelia was thrown into prison and starved to death. That was what was being said.

However, the story that de Brum believed was that Earhart came down on Mili and was taken off to Jaluit. He thought it was highly likely that she and her companion were shipped off to Saipan, because it was the Japanese headquarters. But he had no idea of what ultimately happened.

A few years later de Brum[5] remarked to Brennan's son, Tom, that he wondered why the Americans were still investigating the matter because in his opinion it was over and done with. He noted that the difference between Marshallese and Americans was that his people wanted to forget the days when there were thousands of casualties. Earhart and Noonan were just two more.

De Brum encouraged the senior Brennan to continue his investigation in Saipan, saying that in 1937 Saipan had been the Japanese headquarters for the entire mandated area. The Japanese had facilities there, including airtight security for in-depth interrogations. De Brum also mentioned that the people of Saipan had experienced far more harsh treatment from the Japanese than had the Marshallese. Saipan had been a major producer of sugar, and at one time as many as thirty thousand Japanese civilians had lived there. Even in the early thirties, civil law enforcement agencies were totally dominated by the Japanese.

The older residents still had a deep distrust of foreigners, including Americans. However, the people who were willing to talk about the Earhart affair had told their story many times.

De Brum told Brennan that his family had come from Portugal to the islands in the 1870s. They had purchased a small island with a German partner and had operated a flourishing copra business until the islands fell under Japanese control.

Then de Brum told the following story: He remembered very clearly when he was going to school on Jaluit Island, about the first grade. It would have been in 1937. His father came home one day and informed them that an American lady pilot had been captured and that she was being taken to the Japanese office. People were not permitted to go close to her or come anywhere near where she was captured and taken to the office. His father did not say whether he actually had seen the lady but de Brum distinctly recalled the information he passed on to the family—an American lady had been captured and had been taken to the Japanese high command office in Jaluit.

From all accounts there is a very high likelihood that Amelia Earhart and Fred Noonan were captives of the Japanese on Jaluit in the summer of 1937.

7

Mysterious Missives

"I have been a prisoner at Jaluit, Marshalls, by the Japanese in the prison there. I have seen Amelia Earhart, aviatrix. And in another cell her mechanic, a man, as well as several other European prisoners, held on charge of alleged spying on large fortifications erected on the atoll. Earhart and companion were picked up by Japanese hydroplane."–found in a bottle, October 30, 1938, Soulac-Sur-Mer, France.[1]

FRED GOERNER INCLUDES in his book many odd bits and pieces of information that he received during his investigation of several years. One curious tidbit about Amelia Earhart came from a classified file from the U.S. State Department. He explains that France's state department sent a communication dated October 30, 1938, to the U.S. State Department, saying that a French housewife, Genevieve Barrat,[2] of Soulac-sur-Mer, France, had been walking down a beach and had picked up a bottle with a note in it. The note stated that Amelia Earhart and Fred Noonan were prisoners on Jaluit.

The state department merely filed the communication, but I have noticed that the Saipanese have used it on a map to help promote tourism on their island.

Oliver Knaggs' book, *Amelia Earhart: Her Last Flight,* goes into this unusual story in great detail. Knaggs received a microfilmed copy of the report about the note from the National Archives in Washington, D.C. When he visited the Archives, he was able to see the original report and a copy of the note itself. There were apparently some minor differences between the report about the note and the note itself, but they are not significant.

This is what the report said, as translated: On October 30, 1938, while she had been walking on the beach near Soulac-sur-Mer, on the Atlantic Coast, a Mme. Barrat,[3] age thirty-seven, found a bottle, about half-pint size, stoppered with a cork over which wax had been poured. In the bottle were three items: a lock of chestnut-colored hair, and two pieces of paper with writing in French on them. On one the writer asked God to guide the bottle in order to save his life and those of his companions.

The writing on the other piece of paper stated that the writer was French and had been a prisoner of the Japanese in Jaluit. He said he had seen Amelia Earhart, an aviatrix, and a man he described as her mechanic, and several other European prisoners in separate cells where they were being held on charges of spying.

The writer stated that Earhart and her companion had been picked up by a Japanese hydroplane (seaplane) and according to the Japanese would be serving as hostages.

The writer had been captured after his yacht had been sunk and had been forcibly enrolled as a "stoke hand" on a Japanese ship bound for Europe. His intention was to try to escape when the ship got near the coast. He wrote that the bottle would probably be thrown overboard near Santander, Spain. He hoped that it would arrive in Brittany by September, or at the latest, October 1938.

Barrat delivered the bottle and its contents to the French policemen, who eventually sent it to Paris.

Knaggs also reports that the file containing the bottle note also gave statements by a M. Eric de Bisschop,[4] a former French naval officer currently lecturing on geography.

78

M. de Bisschop declared that on his last trip, in the spring of 1938, he had stopped in Jaluit where he was given a very cordial reception by the Japanese authorities until he indicated that he had passed near Mili Atoll. He stated that then the Japanese looked at him with hostile expressions.

After he was arrested on suspicion of espionage, he was severely and thoroughly questioned for several hours. At the same time, his sailing schooner was searched from bow to stern. But nothing was found and he was freed.

Dwight Heinie

At Jaluit, M. de Bisschop had seen shells for three-inch guns, but did not actually see the guns. He said that the story about Miss Earhart and other people being kept prisoner on Jaluit was possible, but he did not believe it because they would have more likely been drowned "accidentally" than to have been kept prisoners. Natives once told him that a white man who was rumored to be an American spy had visited Jaluit and was found drowned. There were indications that he had been struck over the head first.

As Knaggs read the report, he was struck by the mention of Jaluit and Mili and impressed by M. de Bisschop's comment that the Japanese arrested him when they learned that he had passed close to Mili. Knaggs learned from the photocopy of the original note in the bottle, the exact details of the French brigade which had handled the affair. It also told where the original bottle and lock of hair would probably be found—although it may well have been lost during World War II.

When Knaggs returned to the Marshalls for another visit, he talked with Dwight Heinie,[5] who was convinced that Amelia and Fred had been captured by the Japanese. Heinie said that as a small boy he had heard stories about the lady pilot being taken prisoner by the Japanese. When Knaggs told Heinie the story of the note in the bottle, Heinie said that in 1938, when the big dock was being built, he saw two French yachtsmen taken prisoner.

He also mentioned that there had been a woman who had piloted a plane which had crashed at Mili and that the Japanese had taken her prisoner. But he denied that she had been brought to Jaluit. He also was not familiar with the name of the Frenchman that Knaggs gave to him.

Knaggs also asked the Queen of Mili what she knew about the story of a Frenchman whose yacht had been wrecked at Mili about the same time as the airplane crash. She replied that she had heard talk about a sailing boat which the Japanese had sunk. It had sailed into the lagoon and the Japanese rammed the boat. At first she didn't remember the nationality of the yachtsman, but when Knaggs said he was French, she said she did recall talk about a Frenchman.

Knaggs concludes that he was pleased with what she said. He commented that at least she could vaguely remember the Japanese deliberately sinking a yacht. Her recollection made the message in a bottle which arrived on the French coast that much more believable.

* * *

What are the chances of a bottle thrown overboard off the coast of Spain being picked up on a beach many miles away? Perhaps an oceanographer would be able to answer the question, but the probability of a bottle floating from Spain to France seemed greater to me after one of my Amelia Earhart class members told me about an experience she had. While she was on a ship sailing around South America, the captain suggested that passengers write a note and drop it overboard in a bottle at Cape Horn. She did so. Three and a half years later she received a letter from Madagascar saying that her bottle and note had been found! The time and distance were much greater than those that had been involved in the note in the bottle about Amelia Earhart.

Another mysterious missive, reported by Buddy Brennan, was the photostat of a postcard, purportedly from Amelia, postmarked "Jaluit." This was first reported in a newspaper article written by John Heinie's[6] grandfather for the *Pacific Island Monthly*. Included in the article was a photostat of a postcard that Amelia Earhart may have mailed from the island of Jaluit. Unfortunately, he did not have a copy of the article. He had given it to his cousin, and did not know if it still existed.

Since Brennan's book was written, the article which John Heinie may have had in mind (although it describes a letter, not a postcard) has been located and published in the newsletter of the Amelia Earhart Society of Researchers of May 1991. *The Pacific Island Monthly Magazine,* published in Sydney, Australia, dated May 25, 1938, reads as follows:

"POSTAL MYSTERY, UNCLAIMED LETTER FOR AMELIA EARHART. From: Mr. Carl Heinie,[7] a special correspondent and German Missionary in the Marshall Islands, JALUIT ATOLL, March 17, 1938.

81

"Here is a curious thing. On November 27, 1937 in the Jaluit Post Office, in the Marshall Islands (Japanese), among the unclaimed mail a certain letter attracted my attention. In its upper left corner was printed 'Hollywood-Roosevelt Hotel, Hollywood California.' A little lower down appeared the postal date stamp with 'Los Angeles, California, October 7, 10 P.M.' within the circle. Lower down in the usual place appeared the following startling address:

Miss Amelia Earhart (Putnam)

Marshall Islands (Japanese)

Ratak Group, Maloelap Island, (10)

South Pacific Ocean.

"Written diagonally across one corner was this, 'Deliver Promptly.' On the back of envelope 'Incognito' was penciled in very small, fine handwriting. The letter was unopened, and consequently I have no idea of its contents. Now, it seems to me that anyone in USA writing as late as October, ought to be well aware that Amelia Earhart had been given up as lost long before. Hence, it would appear that the letter may have been written by someone desirous of hoaxing the public. Still, it is just possible that such may not be the case at all.

"Certainly, the writer of the address on the envelope, while making some errors such as anyone at a distance might make, displays a little more geographical knowledge of these parts than one would expect of the average individual, but which one would certainly expect of anyone about to traverse the Pacific, and would be passing this group at a distance of a few hundred miles.

"It is conceivable that Amelia Earhart may have told some trusted friend in America, before setting out on her ill-fated journey, that she intended to take a look-see in at the Marshalls enroute or that she might possibly do so if in any danger as she passed by. And it is possible that this hypothetical friend in Hollywood might think that Amelia had reached this group, and might be lying low for some reason or other at Maloelap. It seems curious that anyone without specific interest in this group should

82

know the name of that particular atoll which is of no great importance. What the number (10) might mean in connection with that island I have no idea."

The editor of the newsletter adds this footnote: "Isn't it coincidental that Margo DeCarie, Amelia Earhart's personal secretary, was living in the Hollywood-Roosevelt Hotel during Sept. Oct. 1937?"

* * *

John Heinie's grandfather's lost postcard and the 1938 newspaper account of an unclaimed letter add to speculations raised by the missive in the bottle more questions that have yet to be answered.

* * *

There is a postscript that needs to be added to this chapter on "mysterious missives." On June 15, 1987, five postage stamps issued by the Marshall Islands, commemorating the Fiftieth Anniversary of Amelia Earhart's attempted flight around the world became the latest additions to the postal aspects of the legend.

One of the stamps, selling for one dollar, shows a map of Earhart's flight from Calcutta, India to the crash site near Barre Island, Mili Atoll, the Marshall Islands.

The remaining four stamps sell for forty-four cents. The first depicts the takeoff of the *Electra* from Lae, New Guinea, as it leaves the end of the runway and starts over the ocean towards Howland Island. The second shows the Coast Guard Cutter *Itasca,* stationed at Howland Island, with black smoke coming from its funnel to make it easier for Earhart to find the island. The third shows the crash at Mili Atoll. Two natives are in the foreground, with the *Electra*, Earhart and Noonan and a rubber raft in the background. The final stamp shows the recovery of the *Electra* by the *Koshu*—with Earhart, Noonan and a Japanese soldier wearing a sword in the foreground.

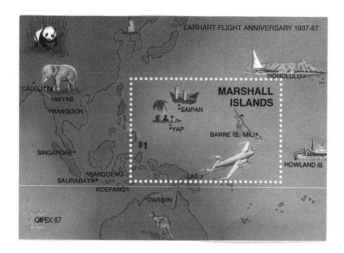

Marshall Islands commemorative stamps

Although the postage stamps do not prove that Earhart crash-landed at Mili Atoll, or was captured by the Japanese, it appears that there is sufficient acceptance by the Marshallese that it happened to merit their issue. Now missives can be sent anywhere in the world from the Marshalls with this portion of the Earhart-Noonan legend succinctly told on an envelope.

84

8

Electra to Emidj

"On the barge was an airplane...It was silver colored...It had two props ..I could not see the tail...I was told that it was the plane an American lady had been flying when she crashed."–John Heinie to Buddy Brennan.[1]

WHEN CALIFORNIA NEWS reporter Fred Goerner visited the Marshall Islands in 1962 he talked not only with Elieu Jibambam but also with Dwight Heinie,[2] then district administrator of education for the Marshalls and president of the Marshallese Congress. Goerner asked Heinie if, in his opinion, it was possible Amelia Earhart and Fred Noonan had been picked up in that area by the Japanese. Heinie replied that it was possible. The Japanese would have been outraged in 1937 to have their secrecy violated. He added that he did not personally know of that incident, but he would believe anything Elieu had said because he consided him to be an honest man.

Dwight Heinie
More than fifteen years later, Oliver Knaggs also interviewed Dwight Heinie.[3] Knaggs describes him as a former administrator of the Marshalls and says that Dwight, who was tall and charming and fluent in English, was fascinated to know they were investigating the Earhart mystery. Knaggs states that Heinie did not have first-hand

evidence to offer about seeing Amelia Earhart in person, although Heinie was on Jaluit at the time and firmly believed that Amelia and Fred had been captured by the Japanese. Heinie told Knaggs that he had heard that there had been a woman who had piloted a plane which had crashed at Mili, and the Japanese had taken her prisoner.

Heinie said he had learned much later that she had been taken to Saipan and later still that there had been a man with her. He also said that he had first learned about the lady pilot from his parents (who later were killed by the Japanese). He also heard from friends that a Marshallese named Bilimon Amaran had given first aid to the man.

Oliver Knaggs then interviewed Elieu Jibambam, with Dwight Heinie serving as translator. It was during this conversation that Heinie made the remark that if the female pilot was flying around there where the Japanese fleet was they might have shot her down.

John Heinie

A few years later Buddy Brennan talked with Dwight's brother John.[4] Brennan described John as a school principal, minister of the local Congregational church and assistant trial lawyer. In 1989 Bill Prymak also interviewed John Heinie.[5] He identifies Heinie (son of Jaluit missionary Carl Heinie) as a prominent attorney in Majuro, well-respected in the community.

John Heinie's story was that during his early life, he lived on the island of Jaluit where he attended Japanese schools. One day, he was just entering high school he believes, the schoolmaster took the students outside, gave them all little Japanese flags, and told them to parade down the harbor wharf. Leaving school in the middle of the day was an exciting event for the students, and when they arrived at the waterfront, they saw that a ship had just pulled into the harbor.

John Heinie did not remember the name of the ship, but he recalled that as they stood there waving their flags, he noticed that the ship was towing a barge with an airplane on it. He could tell that

86

it was silver-colored, even though it was partially covered. The plane was smaller than and did not resemble the Japanese seaplanes with which he was familiar.

John said the plane had two propellers, but he could not see its tail. Maybe it was missing, maybe it was covered up. The plane was held up by the slings coming from the rear end boom of the boat. He did not know what kind of an airplane it was, but later he was told that it was the plane an American lady had been flying when she crashed.

Heinie believed that after the ship left Jaluit, it went on to Kwajalein, then on to Truk and Saipan. From there he thought the ship would go to Japan. Heinie recalled the crash as occuring in the middle of July 1937, because he related it to an event that had taken place in school that year.

In the May 1991 issue of the newsletter of the Amelia Earhart Society of Researchers, Prymak and Gervais write about their visit to the Japanese naval seaplane base at Emidj, eight miles north of Jabor, next to the only harbor in the Jaluit chain of islands. This base was an administrative seat of the Japanese government before and during World War II.

Gervais had shown Prymak what he described as classified pre-strike detail photos of Emidj, the Japanese naval base, taken by a U.S. Air Force reconnaisance plane in July 1942. The photographs showed massive concrete ramps leading into the lagoon, two enormous hangars and several flying boats. But the most important photograph, which was the cause of their trip to Jaluit, was one of a silver airplane behind an operations building. "Intense magnification and scrutiny showed the object to be a twin-engine land airplane, twin-tail, fifty-five foot wingspan, and looking just like a Lockheed *Electra* from an overhead camera shot."[6]

They both wondered why a civilian land-based airplane was at a Japanese naval base in the middle of the war—in contrast to the camouflaged Japanese miliary aircraft there.

87

In Emidj, they found the seaplane ramps still in excellent condition. There were many engines all around and hulks of war vehicles that were rusting. The big hangars were no longer standing. As they started looking for the *Electra*, they found nothing but jungle, and their guides said they would find nothing there. They

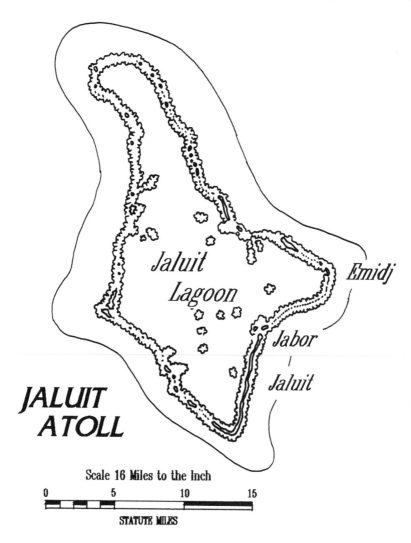

hacked their way to the four corners of the huge hangars where they were shown piles of aluminum aircraft debris that had been bulldozed into one great mass. They were able to identify several Japanese aircraft, but nothing made in the USA.

Kubang Bunitak

But their trip was not completely in vain, as Kubang Bunitak,[6] who had been at Jabor since 1935, spoke of the many thousands of Japanese soldiers and construction workers who had been based both at Jabor and at Emidj. He spoke of a strange-looking airplane that had been unloaded from a naval tender ship onto the Emidj barge, then disappeared from Jabor that night.

"Tokyo"

At Emidj, Prymak and Gervais interviewed a very old Japanese native known as "Tokyo."[7] Through a pastor acting as interpreter, Tokyo explained how he had been brought to Emidj as a labor foreman to run concrete-pouring crews in the 1930s. One day there was great excitement as the weekly barge arrived from Jabor. Normally, it carried construction materials that had been loaded from the larger ships in Jabor Harbor, but this day, there was a special cargo. All work was stopped, and the entire work force was kept off the base. From a distance, Tokyo could see a silver land-type airplane, partially covered by a canvas tarp. The plane was taken off the barge by bulldozers and dragged to a remote area, which was quickly fenced off and camouflaged. Tokyo said the soldiers excitedly discussed this event, but the civilians were forbidden such talk by the threat of severe punishment.

Prymak and Gervais asked Tokyo if he had heard phrases such as "Lady Spy" and "Earhart," but he had not. He could only say that the airplane was not Japanese. He thought that the event had taken place about seven years before the war, which for him would have been the date of the first air raid on December, 1943.

Thus is it quite possible that what he saw had taken place in 1937—the year the *Electra* went down.

9

American Veterans Speak Up

"In the suitcase they found a woman's clothing, a number of clippings of articles on Amelia Earhart, and a leather-backed, locked diary engraved, '10-Year Diary of Amelia Earhart.'"–W.B. Jackson, letter to Fred Goerner.[1]

*T*HE TESTIMONY OF ISLANDERS like Tomaki Mayazo, Bilimon Amaran, John Heinie and Lotan Jack that Earhart and Noonan were taken to Kwajalein on their way to Saipan is supported by information gained from U.S. servicemen who served in the Pacific during World War II.

Chester W. Nimitz

The most prominent of those servicemen was Fleet Admiral Chester W. Nimitz,[2] who gave Fred Goerner encouragement during his investigation. The admiral said that he remembered hearing during the war that some things belonging to Amelia Earhart had been found on one of the islands. Although he couldn't remember which island and hadn't actually seen the material, he stated that Earhart and her navigator had gone down in the Marshalls and were picked up by the Japanese. He told Goerner to contact a general who had commanded a part of the marine forces during the invasion of Kwajalein in 1944, but the general refused to give Goerner any information.

CPO Kelleher

Other servicemen, however, gave Goerner important information. Former Navy Chief Petty Officer J.F. Kelleher[3] told Goerner that he had lived in close contact with the natives in the Marshalls when he had worked for the U.S. military government in 1946. He had heard from four residents of the island of Likiep, Edard and Bonjo Capelli and two individuals known simply as Jajock and Biki, that a plane crash had occurred before World War II. They said that a man and woman, both white, had gone ashore and had been picked up by a Japanese ship. The islanders said that the two had been taken to Kwajalein.

W.B. Jackson

Warren Hasse contacted Goerner about a W. B. Jackson,[4] who had served with the marines during the invasion of the Marshall Islands in 1944. The marines had found some of Earhart's personal effects, said Hasse, who told Goerner that Jackson was a credible witness.

Goerner learned from Jackson that in February 1944, on the Island of Namur, Kwajalein Atoll, Marshall Islands, three marines brought a suitcase from a barracks. They said that the room in which it was found was furnished with a dresser and seemed to be prepared for a woman. They found that the suitcase contained some woman's clothing. There were also a number of clippings or articles on Amelia Earhart. Of particular interest was a leather-backed, locked diary engraved, "10-Year Diary of Amelia Earhart." The men wanted to pry it open, but Jackson explained to them who Amelia was and how the government had searched for a trace of her and said it should be taken to military intelligence. So they closed the suitcase and started toward the regimental command post with it. Jackson never saw or heard of it again.

When Goerner asked Jackson why he had not made his information known before 1964, he replied that he didn't think his knowledge was of sufficient importance and he was not seeking publicity. He had thought that the federal government would have all the facts because the diary and personal effects had been turned over to intelligence.

Victor Maghokian
Another veteran, Victor Maghokian,[5] said he talked to natives on Makin Island in February 1944 through interpreter Rudolph Miller. The islanders said that sometime in the year 1937 a white woman and a white man were in the Kwajalein area for a short time and then were taken away by the Japanese to another island. Maghokian added that one of their men had found a diary and some personal belongings that were supposed to belong to Amelia Earhart.

Three Unrelated Witnesses
An article in the September, 1991[6] issue of the newsletter of the Amelia Earhart Society of Researchers titled, "The Bungalow on Kwajalein," stated that the Amelia Earhart Society "has three unrelated witnesses who have seen or heard of the bungalow in the Japanese barracks at Roi Namor in the Kwajalein chain purportedly set up for a captured lady pilot before the war. The elusive [Amelia Earhart] diary supposedly came from this area. Three separate sources...all containing a common thread."

"Doc" Green
Also in that September 1991 issue, is an article by "Doc" Green,[7] which originally had been published in *Amateur Radio Today*. He writes that in 1944 he was in a submarine rest camp in the Marshall Islands. Green said that American servicemen had managed to talk with some natives who told a fascinating story about a plane which had crashed seven years earlier. The fliers had survived. The woman was uninjured but the man was injured. The Japanese had taken them and their plane to Saipan, according to the islanders.

Ralph R. Kanna

Ralph R. Kanna[8] notified Goerner that as a platoon sergeant of the I & R Platoon, Headquarters Company, 106th Infantry, 27th Division, he had participated in the invasion of Saipan. His duty was to interrogate prisoners.

Kanna said on Saipan the army took a prisoner who possessed a picture showing Amelia Earhart standing near Japanese aircraft on an airfield. Since he thought the picture of the aircraft would be of value, he forwarded it through channels to the G-2, or intelligence, officer. When Kanna questioned the prisoner through one of the Japanese-American interpreters, the Japanese soldier said that the woman had been taken prisoner along with a male companion and that he thought that both had been executed.

The prisoner had been questioned July 5 or 6, 1944, near Garapan. The enemy soldier had belonged to the 118th Japanese Infantry, code no. 11933.[3] Kanna told Goerner he was certain that the photo had been a snapshot, not a magazine clipping, and that it showed Amelia Earhart standing in front of some Japanese aircraft.

Robert Kinley

Goerner also received a letter from Robert Kinley[9] of Norfolk, Virginia, who wrote that he had served with the Second Marine Division on Saipan in 1944. He had found a photograph which showed Amelia with a Japanese officer. The picture appeared to Kinley to have been taken on Saipan.

Although the picture had been lost in July 1944 when a mortar shell exploded nearby, he remembered that it showed Amelia standing in an open field with a Japanese soldier. He believed that the man had worn some kind of combat or fatigue cap with a single star in its center.

Ernest E. Wiles

Ernest E. Wiles,[10] a Honolulu attorney, wrote Goerner that he had served on Tinian Island in 1946. Just a few miles south of

93

Saipan, Tinian had been captured by American forces shortly after they had taken the larger island. In 1946 Wiles had helped repatriate Japanese and Korean civilians from the Marianas. An enlisted man reported to him that one of the internees from Saipan had talked about an American woman who had crashed or landed in an airplane at Saipan before the war. It was not clear to Wiles whether she had been executed or had died from other causes.

Robert Wallack

The television show, "Unsolved Mysteries," on November 7, 1990, presented a dramatized story of Robert Wallack who had served in the First Battalion, 29th Marines. He had been in the second wave going into Saipan in June 1944. One day, when he and his buddies were souvenir hunting, they went through an official-looking brick building where they found a safe. One man, familiar with demolition work, blew off the door of the safe.

At first they thought there was nothing in it, but then Wallack found something—a briefcase which he grabbed. He thought it was packed full of money or something like that. To his surprise it was something he didn't expect to see. He said it was full of Amelia Earhart's papers.

He turned the briefcase and its contents over to his commanding officer but never saw it again. Wallack concluded by saying that he believes that briefcase is still some place in this country. The officer to whom he gave it was of a high-enough rank to know what to do with it. He would know that he had something valuable.

* * *

While none of the reports described above proves conclusively that Earhart and Noonan were in the Marshalls and Saipan, they contribute to a coherent version of the legend about the lost fliers.

10

Saipan Landing

"They were both thin and looked very tired. The woman had short-cut hair, like a man, and she was dressed like a man. The man...had his head hurt in some way."–Josephine Blanco Akiyama to Fred Goerner.[1]

*A*LMOST CERTAINLY Amelia Earhart and Fred Noonan were taken to Saipan from the Marshall Islands. Some natives in the Marshall Islands were told that they were to be taken there. But of even greater significance is the testimony of the many witnesses who saw them on Saipan.

Several of these witnesses told various authors they saw two people who resembled Amelia Earhart and Fred Noonan brought there by plane. Vincent Loomis even suggested in his book the type of plane they could have taken to Saipan–a Japanese Navy seaplane, most likely a Type 91 Hiro H4H1.

The first widely-publicized report of the landing of the two Americans on Saipan came from a former resident of Saipan, Josephine Blanco Akiyama,[2] who had moved to San Mateo, California with her husband and son. She told her story to Captain Paul L. Briand, Jr., an air force pilot, who includes it at the end of his book, *Daughter of the Sky: The Story of Amelia Earhart,* published in 1960.

In April 1960, U.S. Air Force Major Joe Gervais read a summary of Briand's book in the periodical for those in the service,

Stars and Stripes. He then became intrigued with trying to solve the Earhart mystery. While stationed in Okinawa, he immediately offered to help Briand in his research, dedicating his time and energy to the search for clues. Briand agreed to have Gervais and fellow officers assist in gathering information to prove or disprove his theory about Earhart and Noonan's fate. Gervais' early findings and theories are found in Joe Klaas' book, *Amelia Earhart Lives.*

Although Briand had asked Mrs. Akiyama not to tell anyone else about her story, her attorney, William Penaluna, urged her to make it known. He had represented Mr. and Mrs. Akiyama in a war reparations case against Japan for damage done to their Saipan property during the war. In questioning the Akiyamas about their case, he had learned of Mrs. Akiyama's 1937 experience. He believed her and relayed her information to the publisher of the *San Mateo Times.* Her story appeared in the May 27, 1960, issue.

When San Francisco's KCBS news reporter, Fred Goerner, read the article, he was highly skeptical of what Josephine Akiyama[3] had said. Over the years there had been many stories which supposedly had given answers to the Amelia Earhart disappearance. None of them had held up, but he thought that an interview with Mrs. Akiyama would be interesting nevertheless. To his surprise, when he phoned her for an interview, she hung up on him. Apparently the skeptical attitude of other reporters had upset her.

Fred Goerner then got in touch with the newsman, Linn Day, who had written the original article for the *San Mateo Times.* Day was certain that Mrs. Akiyama had told the truth and suggested that Goerner contact her attorney, William Penaluna, for assistance in reaching her.

Thus began Fred Goerner's investigation into the Amelia Earhart-Fred Noonan mystery. After interviewing many people and traveling thousands of miles, he wrote *The Search for Amelia Earhart,* which was published in 1966.

Josephine Blanco Akiyama
This is the story of Josephine Blanco Akiyama, as compiled
from the accounts of Briand and Goerner:

Josephine Blanco Akiyama

In 1946, she, then Josephine Blanco, had been a dental
assistant for an American dentist on Saipan, Dr. Casimir R. Sheft.
Taking a break between appointments, he had talked with a fellow
dentist in the presence of Blanco. In the course of the conversation,
Dr. Sheft casually mentioned the disappearance of Amelia Earhart.
He wondered if she could have ended her flight in the Marianas,
possibly near Saipan. He had read that the marines had found
Amelia Earhart's flight log during the invasion. (Author Briand
comments that it was not the flight log, but rather a photograph
album with Earhart's pictures in it.)

As they were talking, Josephine Blanco suddenly entered into the conversation by saying that nine or ten years earlier, when she was a little girl, she had seen an American woman with hair like a man's, wearing khaki clothes.

Josephine's story, as she would relate it years later, goes like this: She had just finished grammar school, which she had been attending for five years. In March of 1937, she had celebrated her eleventh birthday. She was looking forward to studying with the Spanish missionary sisters in Catholic school. Some of the Chamorro native girls in the Marianas had become sisters, and her priest, Father Tardio had hoped that some day Josephine would become one, too.

One day in the summer of 1937, she was riding her bicycle down the beach road on Saipan, taking lunch to her brother-in-law, José Matsumoto, who worked for the Japanese at their secret seaplane base at Tanapag Harbor on the western shore of the island. As she neared the gate to the base, she saw a large, two-motored silver plane fly overhead and disappear in the vicinity of the harbor. A little later, when she reached the beach area, she found a large group of people gathered around two white people. At first she thought they were both men, but someone told her that one was a woman.

They were both thin and looked very tired. The woman had short-cut hair like a man and she was dressed like a man. The man, she thought she remembered, had his head hurt in some way.

When Briand showed Josephine Akiyama a picture of Amelia Earhart and Fred Noonan, taken on their world flight, she said that the man and woman she saw on Saipan were unquestionably the same as those in the picture. Although the clothes were different, the woman's haircut was unmistakable.

When Fred Goerner interviewed Mrs. Akiyama, he asked her why she had waited so long to tell her story. She replied that she had told Dr. Sheft, for whom she worked, about it on Saipan, back in

1945. Also she stated that she had told U.S. Air Force Captain Briand her story a few months previously.

To check on the validity of her testimony, Goerner telephoned Sheft, who had opened a dental practice in Passaic, New Jersey. The dentist supported her statements and gave his own account of how she had told him about the incident. Sheft said that she would have had no reason for inventing such a story back in 1945.

Sheft had served with the U.S. Navy on Saipan from 1945-46. He had been talking with a navy flier who was having his teeth checked. The discussion led to Amelia Earhart and where she might have been lost in the Pacific. Sheft said at that point Josephine Blanco joined the conversation and told them about having seen two American fliers, a man and a woman, on Saipan before the war.

Sheft told Goerner that although he had given this information to an officer, no one wanted to investigate. Everyone was thinking about getting back to the United States.

Sheft said he didn't bother filing a report, because he thought military intelligence must have been aware of what Josephine Blanco had seen. He remarked that it never occured to him they didn't know this, but apparently that was the case.

The dentist said that years later when he had seen a program about Amelia Earhart on the TV show, "Omnibus," he was surprised that Saipan was not mentioned. He wrote a letter to the producer of the program, but apparently it was too late for him to do anything about it.

* * *

Was Josephine Blanco Akiyama's memory of her experience as a child accurate?

Goerner reports that a navy investigator interviewed Mrs. Akiyama's mother, Mrs. Antonia Blanco,[4] on Guam, about one-hundred-twenty miles south of Saipan. Mrs. Blanco said that her daughter told her about the two American fliers, but she had warned Josephine not to discuss what she had observed with anyone for fear of Japanese reprisal.

99

Thomas E. Devine, who had been with the army on Saipan during the war, in *Eyewitness: The Amelia Earhart Incident*, identifies the investigator who had talked with members of Josephine Blanco's family on Guam as Special Agent Joseph M. Patton. Patton had reported that not only Josephine Blanco's mother,[5] but also a brother (Juan Blanco) and a sister testified that Josephine had told her story long before 1960. Juan had heard the story in 1945 or 1946.

Mrs. Blanco claimed in 1960 that she first heard her daughter's story in 1937. Patton's report states that one day sometime before World War II (presumably in 1937), her daughter came to her shortly after noon, very excited because she had seen a white woman for the first time. Josephine told her that the woman was wearing men's clothes, and had a jacket over her shoulders. Josephine also told her that the woman had been sitting on a bench combing her hair, and that there was an airplane in the harbor. Her daughter did not describe the airplane or mention a plane crash.

Patton concluded that the hearsay evidence of Mrs. Blanco indicated that the woman in question, (Amelia Earhart) may possibly have been brought to Saipan by the Japanese military.

11

Interviews on Guam

"The Japanese took all the clothes off both American pilots and then found out one pilot was an American girl."—Thomas Blas to Joe Gervais.[1]

*I*N JUNE 1960, MAJOR JOE Gervais flew to Guam, intending to continue on to Saipan. However, he was denied permission to go to Saipan for reasons that did not become clear to him until later.

Josephine Blanco Akiyama's Sister

Unable to get to Saipan, Gervais interviewed a number of people on Guam instead. One of them was a Mrs. Bora,[2] forty-five, the eldest sister of Josephine Blanco Akiyama. Guam Chief of Police, Captain José Quintanilla,[3] assisted with the interview. At first Mrs. Bora said that she should not tell anything, because she was afraid she would hurt her sister Josephine in California. But as Quintanilla persisted in his questioning, she said she had heard of the plane crash from Josephine at home. Mrs. Bora was the eldest of ten Blanco children, and had been like a second mother to them (she would have been twenty-five in 1937).

When asked about what Josephine had told her at the time, Mrs. Bora simply replied that Josephine was only eleven then. She was unwilling to say anything more until her husband came home.

101

After Quintanilla gave a lengthly explanation of the harmless purpose of the investigation, Mrs. Bora told what she knew.

Mr. Matsumoto,[4] the husband of one of her sisters, was working at the Japanese military areas as a musician. Her younger sister Josephine had become an errand girl of the family. With her bicycle she traveled freely around the island. On many occasions she took lunch to her brother-in-law, Matsumoto.

Mrs. Bora remembered that Josephine told her family one day something about a plane crash, but she had paid very little attention to it, because Josephine was only eleven. Mrs. Bora was more concerned with duties at home. She was also not interested because the Japanese military were very suspicious of persons who discussed or even knew about such matters. All Chamorros were cautious not to imply at any time that they had any military information. They were afraid that if accused as spies they might be shot or decapitated. They were all afraid of the secret police. People were being shot or getting their heads chopped off during the entire Japanese occupation. Thus she told Josephine to be quiet about what she had said. Mrs. Bora had pushed it out of her mind and could just barely remember that Josephine had said something.

Other Interviews

Police Chief Captain Quintanilla told Gervais that he had talked with Joe Cruz,[5] a member of the Saipan legislature in 1960. Cruz said that about a month before the American naval administration was established, Mayor Benivente of Saipan had selected Elias Sablan, a former mayor of Saipan, to conduct an investigation among the Saipanese people on Guam to find out what they knew about Amelia Earhart. Quintanilla said the investigation had revealed nothing because Jesús Guerrero, who was head of the police during the Japanese adminstration, had told the Saipanese people not to cooperate, and they were not cooperating. Quintanilla said that the Saipanese pretended not to understand the questionnaire that was circulated, and they still remembered how they had been interrogated by the Japanese and later by the Americans, who placed them in compounds after the invasion of Saipan. Cruz also mentioned that a Mr. Patton (this would have been Special Agent Joseph M. Patton) was then on Guam working on the Earhart case.

When Gervais was refused permission from American authorites to go to Saipan, Quintanilla commented that this could be a blessing in disguise, because some of the key people who had been on Saipan in 1937 had moved back to Guam since the end of the war and were available to be interviewed while Saipan was still off-limits.

Quintanilla told Gervais about the difficulties which the people of Saipan had experienced during the previous fifty years. They had been occupied by foreign governments—the Spanish, the Germans, the Japanese, and finally the Americans. As a result of invasions and occupations, there had been many changes of government, languages, and economics. The police chief said the Saipanese, who were Chamorro, showed their greatest loyalty to their senior citizens—people who had preserved a single cultural tradition amidst the changes brought about by various occupying forces.

Quintanilla remembered the oldest living Chamorro who was then on Guam. He believed that if the Amelia Earhart incident had ever taken place she would know about it. If she hadn't seen it, she would at least have heard about it. Quintanilla and Detective Sergeant E.M. Camacho[6] took Gervais to see Mrs. Juana Aquiningo,[7] who was then seventy-nine years old and living with her daughter.

They also interviewed a number of other former Saipan residents now living on Guam. One was José Ada,[8] who was bedridden from a stroke and in his seventies. Although unable to speak, he was able to respond to questioning with gestures. Another was Thomas Blas,[9] who was forty-five-years-old at the time of the interview. In 1937 Blas had been a foreman of a construction crew for Sagami-Sakuroda, a cement company working on new barracks at Chico Naval Base. Forty-six-year-old Pedro Cepeda[10] had been a carpenter working on the housing construction project at the Chico Base at Flores Point in 1937.

Gervais and the two Guamanian police officers used all the following techniques of interrogation: No one was given advance notice of the coming of the team for an interview. No contact was made by a person questioned with the next one to be seen. Interviewees were not given any details or shown photos of Amelia Earhart until after the questioning had been concluded. There was no compensation for information given. Whatever the interviewers learned was volunteered by the individual. Klaas writes that of forty-one persons questioned, only fifteen had information relating to the incident.

Those interviewed told their stories from their own perspective, and, as is to be expected, there were differences in details. But a consolidated and consistent version of their accounts is as follows:

In the summer of 1937, an incident occurred which disturbed the Japanese very much at the time. It happened shortly after noon one day in June or July. The weather was fine; the skies were clear and there was no rain. Some of the workmen had just begun eating their lunch. An airplane came in from the southerly direction of Laulu. As it descended, both airplane motors were running with the propellers turning until it hit the tops of some iron trees in the coffee plantation near the beach. The owner of the plantation was very alarmed by the tops of the trees being broken by the aircraft. The plane went on for a short distance and then crash-landed on the beach about two to three thousand feet from the main Japanese Chico Naval Base at Tanapag Village.

This was very near the Japanese security area around their naval base and seaplane ramps. There were Japanese Navy personnel and other construction workers to the left of the crash. It was so close to the base and the construction that many people began to gather to watch. The airplane was aluminum-colored and had no Japanese marking or insignia on it. At first people were told that an American aircraft had landed with American people in it. Later the Japanese claimed that it was one of their own aircraft that crashed in the area.

The airplane was in fairly good condition on the beach. It was observed later that only at high tide was part of the left wing in the water. The rest of the time, the plane was completely out of the water. The propellers were bent back, but the fuselage and tail appeared to be undamaged. The front of the airplane was punched in with its metal bent and torn.

One flier was observed on the ground lying face down and not moving. The other climbed out of the airplane and approached the flier who seemed injured. When *Kiogan* (Japanese Navy personnel) officers arrived, some with swords, and some soldiers shortly thereafter, they pulled all native construction workers away and told them to stay away. The Japanese also told the local islanders to stay away. They must not observe anything. The military surrounded the pilot standing up. They pushed him back away from the other person on the ground. The standing pilot tried to resist

105

being pushed and was knocked down by a soldier with a gun with a fixed bayonet. While the pilot was on his back, the soldier stood over him. He had his bayonet close to the man's chest so he could not get up.

Observers then noticed the pilots appeared to be American, not Japanese. Both wore khaki-colored flight suits, which looked as though they had been washed many times. The color of their hair was light, typical of many Americans, not black like the Japanese.

When the Japanese took all the clothes off both American pilots, they discovered that one pilot was a woman. The Japanese were very excited about this, saying that the poor Americans had no more men pilots now—they had to use women pilots for military planes.

The Japanese took many pictures of the crash site. The American woman had her hair cut short—just like the other pilot. She wore a long-sleeved black shirt under her flying suit. One of the witnesses had the impression that the woman had flown the two-motor fighter-type airplane.

The Japanese were so agitated by this crash so close to the base that they allowed all construction workers to go home immediately. The entire area was put under tighter security than ever before. The perimeter road the native people were permitted to travel on was closed. They were rerouted through another area farther away which they could not see. Construction workers were immediately taken off the job they had been doing at the base, and put to work in another area far away from the crash site.

One witness, when shown a photograph of the *Electra*, looked at it and commented that the plane that he had seen looked like the one in the photograph and he noted the similarities in the female pilot's haircut to that of the woman in the photograph.

After the Americans landed, Jesús Guerrero, the number-one insular police detective, and other Japanese escorted the American woman and man to the main base. Witnesses reported she appeared to be in her thirties and looked like a man. She was wearing pants, a black shirt and scarf and was carrying a leather jacket. They described her as thin and of average height. Guerrero had told the Saipanese that she was an American spy woman who had taken pictures with a camera hidden in her flying clothes. Guerrero had said she would go to Japan soon.

Four Boys and Their Priest

While Joe Gervais was awaiting permission in 1960 from the American government to continue his investigation on Saipan, he wrote numerous letters to people who had been on Saipan asking if they had seen Earhart and Noonan. He received a letter from a Brother Gregorio, then living on Yap, but who had been a priest along with his brother, Father Tardio, on Saipan in 1937.

Brother Gregorio recalled an event that happened in the late thirties before war was declared. During the summer holidays, some children came to the vestry to tell him that two American spies had been apprehended on Saipan near Garapan. They mentioned one was an American woman who wore long pants like a man and had a haircut like a man. The two Americans were held as spies by the Japanese. The woman's face was very suntanned, like Spanish people's faces. They were taken away by the Japanese for questioning.

Brother Gregorio said that the names of the children were Jesús Rios, Juan Sanchez,[11] José Sanchez, and José Gereyo. He said that Jesús Guerrero had spoken to him a few days later about what he called the two American intelligence spies. But the priest did not know what eventually happened to the two Americans.

The priest continued that after the invasion he'd gone to the U.S. intelligence officer on Saipan. He couldn't recall the man's name, but he asked him if they wanted any information about the two Americans. Brother Gregorio told the officer that a man and a woman had come to Saipan from Hawaii in an airplane to spy for American intelligence before the invasion. The officer was not interested, so the priest left.

A missed opportunity!

107

12

Interviews Flourish on Saipan

"I remember well the lady. Her hair was cut short. Her face, arms, posture–all looked American. But the Japanese kept them. They were very suspicious."–Jesús Boyer to Fred Goerner.[1]

Goerner's 1960 Saipan Visit

AFTER HEARING JOSEPHINE Blanco Akiyama's story in 1960, Fred Goerner decided to go to Saipan to find out what he could about the possible presence of Amelia Earhart and Fred Noonan there. He took Josephine's husband, Maximo Akiyama,[2] who was living in San Mateo, California, with him. Josephine, presumably not asked to go, remained behind. Maximo had no information to support Josephine's story. His father had worked in the Japanese government before and during the war on Saipan, but no mention had ever been made to Maximo about the incident by officials or his wife's family.

On this trip to Saipan with Maximo Akiyama in 1960, Goerner had considerable difficulty obtaining information. Saipan is an island about fifteen miles long and five miles wide at its widest point and in 1960 was part of the Trust Territory of the Pacific under U.S. administration. (It had been taken by American armed forces during World War II.)

There was a secret Central Intelligence Agency (CIA) operation on the northern third of the island training Chinese nationalists to be agents on mainland China.

At that time travel to Saipan was still so highly restricted that Fred Goerner was able to get there only with great difficulty, even when using his credentials as a news reporter. Because the Saipanese saw the CIA's elaborate security measures as similar to those of the occupying Japanese in the thirties and forties, many people were unwilling to give any testimony about events that may have been related to Amelia Earhart and Fred Noonan.

The man in charge of the administration of Saipan in 1960 was Commander Paul W. Bridwell.[3] Because of the CIA operation Bridwell wanted Goerner to see only the unrestricted area of Saipan and suggested that he leave after he had been there for a short period of time.

Bridwell pointed out to Goerner where Josephine had said she had seen the two American fliers. The commander had been on the island for only a month, but he had known Josephine's story for a couple of weeks. He didn't believe it, however. He argued that, if it were true, they would have known about it a long time ago. The navy had been there for a number of years. He had even been on Saipan during the war and had not heard anything about it.

The reporter wondered if Bridwell had questioned any of the natives. Bridwell answered that he hadn't really done so. He had talked with a few of the people that had worked for him, but they didn't know anything. Bridwell then told Goerner that he should be careful about Maximo Akiyama as Akiyma might get together with some of his friends and have them tell Goerner more stories.

Commander Bridwell and Fred Goerner interviewed several Saipanese whom Bridwell had selected. Elias Sablan[4] and Vicente Galvan[5] worked at the land claims office just north of Chalan Kanoa. Now in their fifties, prior to the war both had worked at jobs under Japanese administration. Both were nervous as Bridwell questioned them. Sablan said he did not know of the matter to which they referred. Galvan simply said there was no white lady and man.

Juan Ada,[6] who lived in Chalan Kanoa, and who had been a native judge under the Japanese, said that to his knowledge what they were asking him about did not happen.

Oswald[7] and Manuel Sablan[8] (whom Goerner notes were two more of the many Sablans) had both worked for the Japanese. Oswald said that there was no American or white lady on the island. Manuel said he was sorry, but he did not know what they were talking about—although later he admitted seeing her.

Juan Villa-Gomez,[9] who had served the Japanese at the prison, insisted that there was no white woman or man. He knew nothing about them.

Bridwell had picked the men, he said, because they should know if Amelia Earhart was ever on Saipan. All of them had denied any knowledge of her presence or the presence of any white woman and man there. Goerner wanted to interview more natives, but Bridwell cautioned him to remember that some of the people would tell him what they thought he wanted to hear.

Goerner pondered that statement after Bridwell left him. He observes that there had been something pat about the men they had interviewed that morning. They hadn't liked saying anything. They all had had strong ties with the Japanese or were now working for the U.S. Navy. Goerner wondered if they may have told the commander what they thought he wanted to hear.

Goerner continued with his investigation, however. Maximo Akiyama contacted Josephine's brother-in-law, José Matsumoto,[10] to whom she had taken lunch the day the white American fliers came to Saipan. To Akiyama's delight, he was able to tell Goerner that Matsumoto remembered the incident. He remembered the two American fliers!

Goerner learned that Matsumoto was one of a few Japanese who had been permitted to remain on Saipan after World War II, because he had married a Chamorro woman. He described

110

Matsumoto as a small, sharp-witted but retiring Japanese in his late fifties, who was one of the richest men on Saipan and owned a motion picture house in the village of Chalan Kanoa. Because Matsumoto's wife was Josephine Akiyama's sister, Goerner was not sure how much he could believe Matsumoto.

When Goerner asked Akiyama what Matsumoto remembered and if he had seen Earhart and Noonan, Akiyama replied that he had not seen them, because the Japanese police had taken them away before he got there. But he remembered the people at the seaplane base talking about the incident. He also recalled the Japanese talking about the woman and man fliers. They spoke of them as Americans and spies. When Goerner wondered why he had been so long in telling his story, Akiyama replied that nobody had ever asked Matsumoto before. Goerner himself was able to question Matsumoto later with interpreters, and found that his account was the same as that given to Maximo Akiyama.

* * *

Author Thomas E. Devine supplies additional information not included by Goerner. Clyde E. Holley,[11] a Los Angeles attorney who interviewed Josephine Akiyama in September, 1960, had handled Amelia Earhart's legal affairs. After his interview, Holley wrote Devine what Josephine had said.

In his letter he noted that the thing uppermost in her memory was the fact that the two people were white and she had never seen white people before. He recalled that she was impressed that the woman was wearing pants and had short-cut hair.

Goerner Interviews Other Natives on Saipan

Other Saipan natives provided helpful information to Fred Goerner on his first visit to Saipan in September 1960, before Joe Gervais was allowed to go.

Gregorio Camacho,[12] a farmer from the village of San Roque, had seen the fliers at Tanapag Harbor and later in Garapan. He

111

commented that the Japanese were very surprised to see a woman flier because at the time it was unthinkable that a woman would fly.

Jesús Boyer,[13] also a farmer, who lived in the same village, had been working at Tanapag Harbor and saw the fliers there. He remembered the woman's face, arms and posture. She looked like an American. Her hair was cut short. The incident had been kept very secret. During the time the Japanese were on the island it was very unsafe to disclose information.

Josepa Reyes Sablan[14] was from Chalan Kanoa, a few miles south of Garapan. She had seen the two white people taken into the military police headquarters in Garapan.

Manuel Aldan[15] had not seen the two white people but had heard about them. Also from Chalan Kanoa, he had been a practicing dentist in 1937. At that time his work had been restricted to Japanese officers. It was they who had spoken of the two white people, and had told him that the American man and woman were fliers who had been captured as spies. Aldan said that the officers had made jokes about the United States using women as spies, and said that American men did not have the courage to come and spy themselves.

From Goerner's conversations with more than two hundred Saipanese, he found that the testimony of thirteen of them could be pieced together into a story that seemed to support the account of Josephine Blanco Akiyama:

A white woman and man, Americans and fliers according to what the Japanese had said, either came ashore or had been brought ashore at Tanapag Harbor sometime in 1937. The woman was dressed like a man and had short hair. The man was injured; his head was bandaged. They had been held under guard at the dock area until a Japanese military car arrived from Garapan, just south of Tanapag Harbor, and took them away.

The pair was next seen being taken into the Japanese police headquarters in Garapan. After several hours of interrogation, with a man named Gregorio Sablan serving as interpreter, the woman was taken to Garapan Prison and the man to Muchot Point military police barracks. After being held in prison for only a few hours, the woman was transferred back to Garapan and placed in a hotel that the military police had taken over in 1934 to house political prisoners. Goerner comments that none of the witnesses knew what finally happened to the mysterious white people, although several felt that either one or both of them had been executed.

While this reconstruction of events is based on the testimony of only thirteen witnesses, both Goerner and other investigators found others on Saipan who had more to tell. Some of the Saipanese, who in 1960 denied any knowledge of the white fliers, would later tell what they knew. Nevertheless, the account of events made by Goerner in 1960 served as an excellent starting point for putting together the account of the saga of Amelia Earhart and Fred Noonan on Saipan.

Gervais' 1960 Visit

In mid-December 1960, Joe Gervais was finally able to obtain permission to go to Saipan—a few months after Fred Goerner's visit there. He was accompanied by Air Force Captain Robert S. Dinger and the Guam police chief, Captain Quintanilla. When the party arrived, they were invited to meet Saipan's commanding officer, Captain Paul Bridwell.[16]

Gervais learned that in 1937, Bridwell, as a yeoman on the flagship, *Colorado,* had participated in the first search for Amelia Earhart after she was reported missing. Bridwell was also beachmaster for the invasion of Saipan in 1944 and had spent a total of eight years on the island.

Although a few months earlier Bridwell had told Fred Goerner that he did not believe Earhart and Noonan had ever been on Saipan, he told Gervais and his investigators something different. Bridwell had heard from the natives that the two fliers had been on Saipan, but that they had not crashed there. There had been talk of an American man and woman on Saipan in 1937, but Bridwell said

113

he had not heard of any positive evidence that a plane had crashed there with them in it.

Although Bridwell thought they may have been on Saipan, he didn't think that they had crashed there. Nor was there any evidence that they had been executed there. He gathered from what the natives had told him that a man and a woman who could have been Amelia Earhart and Fred Noonan crashed somewhere else in the Pacific. It was said that they had been apprehended and taken by ship to Saipan, but he had no reliable reports on what happened after that.

Dinger wondered if the navy back in 1937 had searched anywhere else besides the publicized areas for the fliers. Bridwell said that the whole matter was classified and he didn't feel he should talk about it.

The Blancos and Their In-Laws

On this trip to Saipan, the Gervais group spoke with J.Y. Matsumoto,[17] the brother-in-law of Josephine Blanco Akiyama. Matsumoto had told Goerner earlier that he had only heard about the incident, and said the same thing at first to Gervais. But Gervais insisted that Josephine had stated that Matsumoto had seen the crash. With some prodding from Saipan's sheriff, Manuel Sablan, who was also present for the interview, Matsumoto admitted that he had seen the crash. He also stated that the American man and woman were imprisoned. Feeling uncomfortable under further questioning, he refused to say anything more.

The investigators located Josephine's mother, Mrs. Antonia Blanco,[18] who said that she remembered her little girl telling her about the incident. Blanco had told her daughter to keep quiet about it. The mother did not want to know any more because it wasn't safe to know such things in those days. Blanco then stated that Josephine had spoken of the plane crash and the man and the woman in it seven or eight years before the invasion of Saipan. Blanco had not seen the crash, but she did believe what her daughter had told her.

Other Saipanese Eyewitnesses

The Gervais team was also able to talk with Antonio G. Cabrera,[19] a sixty-two-year-old farmer, who owned the land where the Hotel Kobayashi Royokan once had been located. In 1937, Cabrera lived on the main floor of the hotel.

He told investigators that during that time an American woman and an American man lived in the hotel and were under the surveillance of the Japanese. He said that the Americans were only at the hotel for about a week, then were taken away by the Japanese.

When shown a photograph of Earhart, he could not positively identify her as the woman he had seen. However he was certain that he recognized Noonan as the man who had stayed at the hotel. He said he had heard from islander José Camacho[20] that the fliers had crashed in the Tanapag area.

When interviewed, Camacho told Gervais that the plane had crashed in the area next to the Chico Naval Base. His wife added that the two Americans were taken away in a car toward Garapan.

Also confirming the presence of the fliers was José Pangelinan,[21] a merchant in Chalan Kanoa whom Goerner was to interview the next year. Pangelinan said that he saw a white man and woman at the Japanese military police headquarters at Garapan. Someone told him they were fliers and spies. Later he heard that the woman had died and the man had been executed shortly thereafter.

A member of the Saipan legislature, Antonio A. Díaz,[22] who in 1937 had been employed as a chauffeur for the commanding officer of the Japanese Chico Navy Base, was interviewed next. Díaz was one of the very few Chamorro natives who had access to this base. He remembered that one day he overheard a conversation in the sedan between the commander and another Japanese official concerning an airplane that had crashed right next to the base and the two American pilots who were apprehended. One was an American woman. Díaz then suggested that the investigators contact José Basa,[23] who had been employed at Chico Base at the time of the crash.

115

Antonio A. Díaz

At first Basa would not admit that he had seen anything, saying he had been stacking oil drums when the crash occurred. But then, when questioned again with Díaz present and encouraging him, Basa admitted that he had seen the airplane crash and the Japanese arrest the two Americans pilots, one of whom was a woman. He said that after their arrest they were blindfolded and taken away by Japanese officials to Garapan.

The December 1960 activities of the Gervais team of investigators had discovered a number of people who were believed to have information, but who seemed afraid to talk for fear of reprisals. With coaxing, often from a trusted friend or a priest, they had eventually told what they knew.

Goerner's 1961 Visit

On September 7, 1961, Fred Goerner began his second trip to the island in the Marianas, this time alone.

Commander Bridwell

He again met with Commander Bridwell.[24] Goerner found to his surprise that the island administrator was not as skeptical as he had been the previous year about reports that Earhart and Noonan had been on Saipan before the war. Goerner learned Bridwell had heard more testimony from natives on Saipan, and as a result seemed more open minded about what might have happened.

Bridwell told Goerner that he thought there was a lot to the natives' story. There undoubtedly had been a couple of Americans, a man and a woman, on Saipan before the war, and they were not there on a friendly visit.

Bridwell indicated to Goerner that, although the descriptions fit the missing fliers, he did not believe that Earhart had flown her plane to Saipan. He said conversations he had heard while he was in the vicinity of an admiral's office in 1937 made him think Earhart and Noonan could have possibly gone down in the Marshall Islands. Bridwell was unwilling to identify the admiral, but he did state the reason for the belief that they had crashed in the Marshalls.

Bridwell suggested that Goerner forget Saipan and switch his investigation to the Marshalls for several reasons. First, the Marshalls are close to Howland Island. Second, the Japanese had been very secretive about the Marshalls, particularly Jaluit and Kwajalein. Third, there had been some reports from natives during the Marshall Islands invasion that a white woman pilot had gone down in the area before the war.

Goerner speculated that the testimony of the natives of Saipan indicated Earhart could have been brought there by the Japanese, and Bridwell agreed that that was possible. Bridwell noted that Japan had regular military seaplanes going to Saipan from the Marshall and Caroline Islands. The fliers could have been brought by ship, however.

117

The Sanchez Brothers

During this Saipan visit, Goerner learned also about the experience of Brother Gregorio, who had written Major Joe Gervais in the previous year. Saipan's Father Sylvan Conover had spoken with Brother Gregorio at a recent church meeting, about the testimony of the Sanchez brothers.[25]

Goerner and Father Sylvan attempted to get first-hand confirmation of their story from the Sanchez brothers themselves, who worked as mechanics for the National Technical Training Unit (NTTU), which was the CIA operation on Saipan. Although they were surprised and disturbed about what Brother Gregorio had said, they admitted they had some knowledge of the incident. They promised to come to the church mission house the next day to give details, but wanted to refresh their memories before making a definite statement.

The next morning only one Sanchez appeared. His attitude had completely changed—he claimed neither he nor his brother had any helpful information. He said that Brother Gregorio did not remember correctly. They knew nothing of what he said. Thorough questioning by Father Sylvan brought no results.

Goerner comments that the Sanchez brothers were obviously frightened. They were not going to say anything. The next year Goerner was to learn that they had been told by the navy or NTTU not to cooperate with the people who were asking questions about the missing fliers.

Goerner's 1962 Visit

When Goerner returned to Saipan in 1962, he found that the CIA operation had ended.

Vicente Galvan

He then happened to encounter Vicente Galvan,[26] an islander he had talked with two years earlier. (Devine states that his real name was Vincente Guerrero.) In 1962 Goerner found Galvan was

118

a changed man. As Goerner was walking along the main Chalan Kanoa road toward the Mission House, Galvan pulled up in his jeep and politely offered Goerner a ride. With Goerner at the time was José Quintanilla,[27] the chief of police of the island of Guam.

Galvan, whose English had improved remarkably, apologized for his responses to questions two years previously. Other witnesses had also not been helpful, he said. He explained that in his search for the woman flier, many who knew of her had not helped Goerner. For some, it was to protect their jobs. The navy and NTTU wanted Goerner to be discouraged. Others had been afraid to speak. The Japanese were very hard with people who talked, and there still were Japanese sympathizers on Saipan.

Galvan then continued that the woman they were looking for, along with a man, had been picked up by the Japanese in the Marshall Islands. He had heard this from Japanese officers. Many others knew about this. He told Goerner to check with several natives of Saipan whom he mentioned by name.

Goerner commented that he had talked with two of them in 1960 and wondered if someone had gotten to them too. Galvan replied that those people he mentioned knew it was not wise to give information. Perhaps they would be willing to talk now—it would be worth a try.

Galvan said that it was possible that the woman and perhaps the man were brought to Saipan from the Marshalls, but they had not flown their plane to Saipan.

When Goerner inquired about the fate of the *Electra,* Galvan suggested that he talk with Antonio Díaz, who knew a lot. He had been a driver for the Japanese commanding officer at Tanapagchico Base. Goerner then asked what happened to the man and woman after coming to Saipan. Galvan offered the opinion that it was possible they did not leave the island.

Why had Galvan been so helpful in 1962 when he had been uncooperative two years before? According to Goerner, Father Sylvan had proudly explained Vicente's sudden cooperation. He

119

had been given a decoration by the pope, because two of his daughters were nuns and one of his sons had recently been ordained a priest. Galvan's intention now was to live up to his children's reputation and expectations of him.

At one point in Goerner's conversation with Galvan, José Quintanilla said that the woman they were concerned about was held by the *Kempeitai* (secret police) at Kobayashi Royokan in Garapan. He said that the Japanese had taken over the hotel in 1936 to house important prisoners. The Chamorran woman who owned the property lived on Guam at the present time. Galvan knew her; she was Concepcion ("Chande") Díaz. Quintanilla[27] had questioned her in 1960 when two air force officers (presumably Gervais and Dinger) had been making investigations on Guam. She said the Japanese held a woman as a spy sometime in 1937 and 1938, and the description she gave matched Amelia Earhart.

Near the end of their conversation, Vicente Galvan told Goerner that he should talk to many more people, including Joaquina Cabrera, who had done laundry work at the Kobayashi Royokan Hotel, where many political prisoners had been kept.

Goerner and Devine's 1963 Visit–Mercaria Wabol

In 1963, Fred Goerner made his final trip to Saipan. One of the men accompanying him was Thomas E. Devine, who years later was to write about this trip and other experiences in his own book. On the 1963 visit, Devine listened to Father Sylvan Conover interview Mecaria Wabol,[28] whom Fred Goerner does not mention. Devine writes that Wabol remembered that when a plane landed on Saipan, a white woman remained in the plane for a long time. When a man emerged from the plane, he was seen to have a bandage wrapped around his head.

Late 1960s Visits of Don Kothera's Team

In 1967, three men from Ohio flew to Saipan with the intent of finding the *Electra*. Don Kothera had seen a plane on Saipan

120

when he was stationed there in 1946 and he wondered later if it might have been the Earhart plane. Kothera, Ken Matonis and John Gacek were successful in finding parts of a plane that was probably the one Kothera had seen in 1946, but they were not successful in making a positive identification. They were, however, able to interview witnesses on this trip. The three made a second trip a few months later, with two other men—Jack Geschke and Marty Fiorillo. It was their intention to find the Earhart-Noonan grave, based on the information they had received earlier from one witness. After their return, Joe Davidson wrote a book about their experience, *Amelia Earhart Returns From Saipan.*

A man with a different story of Amelia on Saipan was Louis Igatol.[29] He told the men that when he reported to work one morning, an official car drove inside the Tanapag Harbor seaplane base. Inside the car was an admiral and a woman. When Igatol was shown a picture of Amelia Earhart, he said she was the woman he remembered, although she had worn different clothes from those in the picture. She "was skinny and had short hair," "looked very tired and hurt a little bit." His wife remembered the year as being 1937. This was the only white woman that Igatol had ever seen on the island.

Author's 1991 Visit

On my own visit to Saipan in April of 1991, Manny Muña and I looked at the names of the people of Saipan mentioned in Tom Devine's book, *Eyewitness: The Amelia Earhart Incident,* published in 1987, which I had with me. Many of these names Devine attributed to Goerner's book, *The Search for Amelia Earhart,* published in 1966, which I did not have with me. Muña brought me up-to-date on most of the people whose interviews I have reported in this book and on some of their contemporaries as well.

Muña: "All these people I know. Gregorio Camacho is dead. Jesús Boyer is dead. Jesús Bacha Salas is dead. Josepa Sablan is dead. Manuel Aldan—there are two Manuel Aldans. This is the problem.

121

They have the same last name. They are different middle names. Assuming he's talking about Manuel Aldan, the dentist, he's still alive.

"These are all my neighbors in Chalan Kanoa. Antonio Díaz is my first cousin. He's dead. José Ríos Camacho is now in Los Angeles. He's around seventy-years-old by now. Juan Reyes is dead. Pedro Sakisag—this guy in Rota now. Maria Ohasi—this lady is still here—still alive. She is about eighty-eight-years-old. Francisco Tudela— there are two Francisco Tudelas. I don't know which one they are talking about. José Basa is dead. Mrs. Akiyama's brother-in-law, José Y. Matsumoto is still alive."

I asked Manny about his work with the CIA, and this is the conversation we had:

Muña: "I worked for the U.S. Naval Communications. We received and sent messages. We were on a relay station—receiving a message from one station and sending it to the other station. I operated the radio teletype and I also used the International Morse Code. During the time the navy was here they called it NTTU (National Technical Training Unit). It was a part of the CIA, and you cannot speak about the CIA. I recall one time in 1957 when the United Nations had a visiting mission. It included the Russians. They posed a question as to why the people of Saipan and Tinian were governed by the military rather than the civil government. The Russians went back to the United Nations and asked the question there. President Kennedy eventually signed an executive order to transfer the islands from the Department of the Navy to the Interior Department. This was to be more consistent with the international treaties."

Muña told me of an incident which deepened his interest in the Amelia Earhart-Fred Noonan mystery.

"After several years when I was working for the CIA I saw a news clipping from the *Washington Post*. It claimed that Amelia Earhart was shot down on Saipan and was imprisoned on Saipan for several years. I had to find out whether the story was true because

Mrs. Blanco Akiyama in 1960 said that she remembered that a woman flier, and a man, were captured in Saipan in 1937. Mr. Mayberry was the transportation officer for the CIA. I worked for the CIA for four years. When he received the clipping from his brother in Washington, who was also working for the CIA, he asked me to see if this was true or not. I said we would have to do further research.

"They wanted to know about the plane that went down in Tanapag Harbor. At that time I had a small fishing boat. Mr. Mayberry, two other people and I went diving. The two people in Tanapag knew where there was a plane in the water. But it was not the Amelia Earhart plane. It was an airplane the Japanese shot down. The American pilot was from the USS *Bunker Hill*. This was a carrier. The plane was a dive bomber."

Wilson: "So the plane in Tanapag Harbor was a U.S. plane that was shot down in 1944?"

Muña: "During the invasion. There was one Saipanese who mentioned that she saw Amelia Earhart and Fred Noonan in 1937. Many people here at that time didn't even know anything that really happened. But they did know that there was a woman and man who were blindfolded in 1937. But they did not know who they were or where they had come from."

Wilson: "Now what was it that Mrs. Akiyama said?"

Muña: "In the news clipping? She said she went to the store, and remembered when they blocked the road to let these people pass through. They were riding on a sidecar of a motorcycle. She saw a woman and a man who were blindfolded and they said that they were shot down in Tanapag Harbor. That's what she said."

Wilson: "That's what *she* said. She was incorrect then."

Muña: "She might not be. She might have gotten off a ship in Tanapag Harbor."

I wondered about the possibility of finding official documentation of the presence of Amelia Earhart and Fred Noonan on Saipan.

123

Wilson: "The Japanese government has never admitted that she was shot down or captured. You would think that after all this time in the interests of historical accuracy they might come forth with some statements. But again that would require extensive research.

"I'm trying to determine whether there would be some records somewhere. Also, would there not be some records here on Saipan, at one time, of the prisoners who were kept in prison? Wouldn't the Japanese have these unless they were destroyed during the war?"

Muña: "Well, you were a marine and you know the devastation on this island after the war. Some of the villages were untouched because the commander of the invasion of Saipan was aware that the Chamorro people were living in Garapan. And there was the bombardment of Garapan City. All the people there were Catholic, you know. They decided not to touch it. But after they found out there were no Chamorros living in Garapan City any more they started to bulldoze the houses. Whatever was standing during that time in Garapan they pushed it down—everything. If they hadn't destroyed it by bombing they did by bulldozer."

Wilson: "So only the jail and the hospital have survived to a certain degree?"

Muña said yes, along with a few things such as a statue of the man responsible for the sugar cane industry on Saipan. He also told me about the government of Saipan and the part he (Muña) played in it.

Muña: "I was one of the negotiators for the covenant that established the Commonwealth. During that time we were very enthusiastic about being a part of the American family. We introduced a measure to establish what they call the Marianas Political Status Commission. We opened the door between the U.S. government and the Northern Marianas government so that we could be a part of the American family.

"After the war Saipan and the rest of the Marianas were under the Trust Territory umbrella. There were several districts, like the

Marshall Islands. Ponape. Yap. Palau. They were under the U.S. Trust Territory. During that period, when I was in the Congress of Micronesia, every district has moved progressively to become a separate and independent state—you know from other districts.

"We lobbied senators and congressmen to pass the covenant. Some were very receptive and sympathetic. Some were not.

Wilson: "Now you say Vice President Bush came on the island?"

Muña: "Oh yes. In 1985 he came here and visited the island. He stayed over just one night. Indeed we had a big reception up in the Governor's House. VIP people were invited. It so happened I met in person Vice President Bush.

"I met President Ford also in person in Washington at the signing of the covenant in the Oval Office. This occured March 24, 1976. I won't forget the date when we were in that office. We have March 24 as our legal holiday for the Commonwealth. We call it 'Covenant Day.'"

* * *

Few people today realize that Saipan (part of the Commonwealth of the Northern Marianas) is a part of the United States, where English is spoken, where U.S. currency is used, where there is a U.S. post office and a telephone area code similar to those used on the mainland!

Manny Muña's personal and official connection with the history of the Marianas give him considerable stature locally and internationally. His intimate knowledge of Saipan in the 1930s and his close acquaintance with the eyewitnesses to Earhart and Noonan's presence there make him a highly credible source of information about the legends concerning the lost fliers.

13

Hotel for Political Prisoners

"They were there...a white lady and man. The police never left them. The lady wore a man's clothes when she first came. I was given her clothes to clean. I remember pants and a jacket. It was leather or heavy cloth, so I did not wash it. I rubbed it clean. The man I saw only once. His head was hurt and covered with a bandage, and he sometimes needed help to move."– Joaquina Muña Cabrera to Fred Goerner.[1]

Antonio M. Cepada

ON THE ISLAND OF GUAM in 1960, Gervais interviewed Antonio M. Cepada,[2] a fifty-two-year-old employee of the Buick garage at Agana—the capital.

Cepada said that one summer about two years after he got married, he saw an American girl who was referred to by some as "the American spy woman." She had been assigned to the second floor of the Hotel Kobayashi Royokan in the summer of 1937. He did not remember any plane crash. But he did see the girl twice on two separate occasions outside the hotel over a period of two months.

Cepeda saw her outside the hotel when he went to work. The hotel was located in East Garapan Village. He said the girl wore unusual clothes—a long raincoat belted in the center. It was a faded khaki. Her height was average for an American girl. She had a thin

126

build. Her hair appeared to be reddish-brown and was cut short like a man's hair—trimmed close in the back like a man. She did not wear powder or lipstick.

Antonio M. Cepada

He was not aware of how she had been captured. Rumor was that she had taken secret pictures with a hidden camera in her flying suit. He saw her only twice and thought that she might have been deported to Japan. He said the woman looked soft and was very calm. She did not smile, and her thoughts seemed to be far away. He believed that she did not notice her surroundings and the people much. He believed that she was about thirty-five years old. Everyone on Saipan then referred to her as Tokyo Rosa. In 1937, the name, "Tokyo Rosa" meant "American spy girl." She was not the same person as the Tokyo Rose who had broadcast on the Japanese radio during the war.

127

When Gervais showed Cepada a photograph of Amelia Earhart, he asked if it looked like the girl he had seen twice on Saipan. Although Cepada did not know her name, he recognized the picture as being the same as the woman he had seen.

Carlos Palacious

Carlos Palacious[3] before the war had been a salesman for the Ishi-Shoten, a merchandise store located near the Hotel Kobayashi Royokan in East Garapan Village. Palacious told them that he had seen the woman only twice in about a three-month period. It was while he was going to and from the store where he worked. The first time he saw her was at a window on the second floor of the hotel. The window was open, and she had on what looked to him like a man's shirt with short sleeves and an open collar. The girl had short dark reddish-brown hair, cut like a man's hair in back. He couldn't see any makeup or lipstick. The second time he saw the girl she was standing at the entrance to the hotel. She wore the same white shirt and dark skirt, and American-type woman's shoes. It was the same person that he had seen on the second floor. She had a trim figure.

Palacious said he had no knowledge of the crash or other details leading to the woman's imprisonment. He said that he didn't know where the girl had been captured. He never heard anything about a crash. All he heard was that Tokyo Rosa was an American spy girl and that she had taken secret pictures. He commented that Tokyo Rosa was his people's expression for an American spy girl.

He said the woman appeared to be thirty-four to thirty-six years old. He didn't know what happened to her but thought she was probably deported to Japan. Gervais then showed a photo of Amelia to Palacious, who confirmed the resemblance. As had Cepeda, he said he had never heard of Amelia Earhart by name.

Joaquina M. Cabrera

In 1962, Fred Goerner interviewed Manny Muña's sister, Mrs. Joaquina Muña Cabrera.[4] Goerner felt that her testimony brought him closer to learning the truth about the woman held at Kobayashi Royokan than any other witness.

Mrs. Cabrera said that she had done laundry for the Japanese and for the prisoner who stayed there in 1937 or 1938. She said that one day when she came to work a white woman and man were there. The police never left them. The woman wore men's clothing when she first came. Joaquina was given her clothes to clean. She remembered pants and a jacket made of leather or heavy cloth, so she did not wash it, but rather rubbed it clean.

Joaquina Muña Cabrera

She saw the man only once, and did not wash his clothes. His head was hurt and covered with a bandage, and he sometimes needed help to move. The police took him to another place, and he did not come back.

129

Mrs. Cabrera described the lady as thin and very tired. Every day more Japanese came to talk with her. She never smiled to them but did to her. Although she did not speak the Chamorro language, Joaquina knew the woman thanked her. She was a sweet, gentle lady. Mrs. Cabrera thought the police sometimes hurt her because she had bruises, and at one time she held her hurt arm at her side. Then, one day the police said she was dead of disease.

When Goerner asked if she was sure she had died of disease, Joaquina Cabrera simply acknowledged that that was what the police had said.

Father Arnold Bendowske, who was present for the interview, asked Mrs. Cabrera to describe the woman. She replied that she was tall for a woman, and her hair was short like a man's. But she had a thin, pretty face with a look of kindness and suffering.

However, she had not seen the man as well because of the bandage. All she could remember was that he was tall and thin.

She said that the woman was in custody for a long time before she died. She wasn't sure, but it was for many months—perhaps a year.

When Goerner asked what happened to the man, Mrs. Cabrera responded that she had heard he also died. When asked if he had died or was killed, she answered simply that he was just dead. The woman may have been buried near Garapan, but Joaquina Cabrera was not certain.

* * *

Buddy Brennan also talked with Joaquina Muña Cabrera[5] when he visited Saipan a number of years after Goerner's visit. Manny Muña told Brennan that he might learn something from his sister, because she had worked inside the prison compound for a time and did laundry for the woman they believed was Amelia Earhart.

Brennan describes his visit with her by writing that the old lady was enormously pleased to see her brother and treated his group like royalty. Manny patiently led her through the time she worked at Garapan Prison for the Japanese. She did her best but at her age she was having some difficulty. At times her story was completely clear; at other times she could not keep events in sequence. Nevertheless her memory about the woman was keen, for she had shown kindness toward Joaquina Cabrera, and that had made an indelible impression. She could describe her physical features in a credible way but was unable to give accurate dates.

* * *

In 1991, I asked Manny Muña to talk about his sister, Joaquina Muña Cabrera, and her contacts with Amelia Earhart. He said, "Even my sister made a statement. At first she said she never saw Amelia Earhart because she was afraid. But after she knew her rights she made a statement."

We had several conversations regarding his sister. Muña said that she worked for the Japanese officer who was in charge of the prison in Saipan. She also worked as a maid. Every afternoon, she took lunch to her boss who worked at the prison. She saw a woman and a man in the prison cells she had to pass on her route. She tried to find out who the woman was, and the man with whom she talked thought the woman had come from some place like America.

Because Joaquina had not spoken English, she did not try to talk with the woman but had just looked at her. Manny said that his sister was still living at the age of ninety and was in such good health that she could still run. "She doesn't even need eyeglasses for crocheting," he said proudly.

While looking through Tom Devine's book with Muña I pointed out a picture taken by Devine of a bombed-out two-story structure in Garapan. I asked Muña if he could identify it and he said it was a hotel—the Kobayashi Royokan, the hotel at which his sister said she had seen Amelia Earhart. Cabrera said she also had seen Earhart later in prison.

Muña mentioned that the hotel was near the prison—no more than six hundred feet away. He described the kind of work that his sister did at the hotel as well as working for the chief of police at the prison. "She worked four hours on that job and four hours at her other job."

Muña commented that when Fred Goerner was on Saipan interviewing witnesses, he had shown a photograph of Amelia to his sister and said that Joaquina identified her as the woman she had seen on Saipan for a long time.

14

The Ring and the Book

"She sat right next to me and, as I was writing on the map, she took my pencil; then she pointed out to the islands that I should note on the map. She gave [my sister] the ring. The stone was white...and...[the setting] was white gold. "–Matilda Fausto Arriola to Father Arnold Bendowske.[1]

MATILDA FAUSTO ARRIOLA[2] was first interviewed by the Joe Gervais team in 1960. At first unwilling to say much, she eventually trusted the investigators with her story. The next year Fred Goerner also interviewed Matilda[3] on Saipan in 1961. She was also interviewed by Don Kothera and his team in 1967.[4]

She had been born of a Japanese father, who worked as a tailor, and a Chamorran mother–Hosepa Díaz Fausto. Before and during World War II, she had lived in Garapan. The Kobayashi Royokan Hotel, where the Japanese *Kempeitai* used to house political prisoners, was next to her home. For many months in 1937 and 1938, she had seen the white woman whom the Japanese referred to as both a flier and a spy.

When Oliver Knaggs returned to Guam in 1980, after his trip to the Marshalls, he tried to see Bishop Felix Umberto Flores of Guam for information about Earhart-Noonan eyewitnesses. Although the bishop was out of town, he had left Knaggs a folder containing transcripts of Bishop Flores' translations from Chamorro to English of Father Arnold Bendowske's interviews which had been conducted in November of 1977. Vincent Loomis noted that there were well over two hundred interviews with Saipanese witnesses in the files. Many were confusing; some were consistent. Knaggs quoted some of the interviews verbatim in his book, commenting that the Chamorros were very religious folk and it was most unlikely that any of them would dare make up a story given to a priest. Thomas Devine states that the interviews with the Saipanese about Earhart's presence on the island had been requested by Rear Admiral Kent J. Carroll of the Pentagon. Copies of the transcript were sent to both Carroll and to Devine.

Bishop Felix Umberto Flores

Knaggs reprints the transcript of an interview conducted by Father Arnold with Matilda Fausto Arriola.[5] Mrs. Arriola mentioned that she had been previously interviewed by Goerner, although she had forgotten his name. The priest told her that Admiral Carroll of the Pentagon had asked Bishop Flores to have her interviewed on tape because she had actually seen Amelia. Although there were some inconsistencies in the four interviews, the following story emerges:

In June or July 1937 or 1938, when the fruit was in season, an American woman stayed at the military-operated Hotel Kobayshi Royokan. At that time Matilda was a young girl living with her family next door to the hotel. She saw the American woman in the hotel.

Matilda Fausto Arriola

She never saw an American man with her, although she believed the woman had a husband. She did not know the woman's name, what kind of work she was involved in or why she had come to Saipan. The woman did not mention her name nor who she was. The American woman was tall and very thin, with short brunette hair cut like a man's, although slightly longer. Her face was that of a very strong woman.

The first time Matilda saw her, the woman was wearing men's clothing, but later she was given a woman's dress. She was dressed in what Matilda called a cloth trench coat. The first time the young girl saw the woman, she looked very pale as though she were sick. She wore no makeup. The woman came to the family house and looked at it when she was coming from or going to the outside toilet. The house was located between the hotel and the outside toilet. Matilda and her sister offered the woman food. She accepted it but ate very little, only some fruit.

She saw the woman many times. Each day she would come out into the yard and walk around it. Two detectives watched the hotel daily, keeping the American from coming and going as she wished. She gave her fruit several times. The guards did not prevent her from doing so. Matilda's English was too limited to carry on a conversation with the woman.

The next time the American woman visited from the hotel, she had burn marks and bandages on her left forearm. There were also bruises or burns on the right side of her neck. She thought the burns might have been caused from cooking by oil. Matilda was working on her geography lesson for school. She was writing something, doing her homework about the islands of the Marianas and the rest of Micronesia. When Matilda opened a map, the woman sat next to her. As the young girl was writing on the map, the woman took Matilda's pencil and the book from her and pointed out an island on a map of the Pacific Ocean. Then she said something in English which Matilda did not understand and she signaled she ought to put a name there. (Another Saipan woman interviewed, Maria Roberta Dela Cruz,[6] having heard Matilda's story, stated that the woman had taken a pencil to indicate on a map where the island was that her

136

plane went down.) Unfortunately, the book was lost in the destruction when the island was invaded in 1944. Afterwards, she helped Matilda with her geography homework. At the house there was broiled breadfruit and they offered her some to try. The woman ate a little. The family offered fresh fruit from the kitchen. The woman did take some fruit but she had to go back to the hotel.

Matilda thought probably the woman had some kind of problem with diarrhea. Then she came back again that same evening. The woman talked with Matilda's mother, and also with her brother, Felipe, who was leaving the house with his textbook materials—probably to study with a classmate. Matilda did not know what the topic of conversation was. When the woman left, both Matilda and her mother thought that she looked sick.

A hotel servant once came to Matilda's house asking for fruit but didn't say for whom. Matilda's father got some fruit from the ranch—pineapple, mangoes, and laguana—and sent them to the hotel.

One day the woman came out in the yard and she looked very sick and sadder than usual. Matilda gave her a piece of fruit and the woman smiled. Then she gave Matilda's sister, Consolacion (Fausto Arielo), a ring from her finger and put her hand on the girl's hand in friendship. The ring had a single pearl in a white gold setting. When Matilda's sister was sick, she took the ring off of her finger and gave it to Matilda, who took care of it until after the war. And then Inointion Trinidad Tenaio, the daughter of her brother, borrowed the ring when they went to Truk and it was lost there.

Although Earhart's family apparently has not confirmed that she owned such a ring, Goerner believes it is possible she could have purchased the ring on her trip. However, no photographs exist that show Amelia wearing it.

This was the last day that Matilda saw the woman. As she left, she held Matilda's hand very tightly. The next day a busboy who worked at the hotel came and asked Matilda's family to make two wreaths. Since this meant there had been a death, Matilda asked him who died. The servant gave a vague reply, so Matilda assumed it must have been the woman who her mother said was American.

When Matilda asked what had happened to her, the busboy said she had died of dysentery. Matilda asked the servant how they knew she had died. He said the bed on which she had slept was soaked with blood. They had found her other gown stained with the effects of dysentery.

The servant then paid for the wreaths, made with artificial flowers, and took them. As there was no black ribbon the half-English wife of a local official obtained the black ribbon for the two wreaths.

When Gervais showed Matilda several photographs of Amelia Earhart she said that they looked like the woman she saw. Later, Goerner showed Matilda pictures of fifteen different women, including Amelia Earhart, clipped from various newspapers and magazines. Matilda picked one of Earhart, saying she was sure that was the woman, but that she had looked older and more tired. She also noticed the hair she saw in the picture was very, very short but when the woman had come to the house, it had appeared longer.

While the stories of the ring and the book are fascinating, they are more examples of legends that cannot be proven without evidence. As with previous testimony, we must draw our own conclusions about the accuracy of the memories of the witnesses and their integrity. Yet, what they have said may well fit into a pattern of events that really did happen.

15

Cells No. 1 and 4

"What Mr. Salas said was this. He was in cell No. 2, and the other prisoner from Saipan was in cell No. 3. He was very much aware of when the two prisoners–Earhart and Noonan–came in. If Fred or Amelia tried to talk to each other they had to shout. When Amelia shouted to Fred, Fred would answer. When Fred shouted to Amelia, Amelia answered. So this is how Mr. Salas knew who was Amelia and who was Fred."–Manny Muña to author, 1991.

"I looked at her several times but I did not have a chance to be real close to her because the Japanese were constantly watching me. I was afraid because the Japanese can really give some punishment. She was an American. I saw her at least three times."–Anna Villagomez Benavente to Father Arnold Bendowske.[1]

Ramon Cabrera

WHILE ON GUAM IN 1960, Gervais and Quintanilla had interviewed a former guard at the Saipan prison, forty-one-year-old Ramon Cabrera,[2] who remembered two American prisoners in the late summer of 1937.

Cabrera recalled that two American fliers were blindfolded, bound and brought to the prison. They both wore khaki-colored flying suits, and one had a heavy growth of whiskers. He described the other as a strange-looking American man with no whiskers and a smooth face. The one without whiskers was smaller in height, thin in body, and had lighter skin. Both were dressed the same and both had short haircuts. They were kept in separate cells at night, but were permitted to exercise out in the main prison yard for short times during the day. There were about two hundred prisoners in the prison at the time.

He continued that for the first three or four days the two could not seem to eat their prison food. Cabrera said that it was very bad. He wouldn't even eat it himself unless he had been forced to do so. Cabrera recalled that about the fourth day they began to eat even though they didn't like breadfruit and other bits thrown in. They fed the prisoners three times a day. But this was only one-third a regular meal-size portion. This meant prisoners got only one full meal a day.

Gervais wanted to know if one of the two American fliers was a woman. Cabrera, surprised by the question, answered simply that there were two American pilots. Cabrera didn't know what happened to them. Gervais speculated that they might have been deported or executed, as they were taken away.

Ana Villagomez Benavente

Father Bendowske's interviews continue to bring up more accounts the islanders told about the fate of Earhart and Noonan—including the fliers' imprisonment.

Knaggs writes that after talking with Matilda Arriola, Father Arnold Bendowske interviewed Ana Villagomez Benavente,[3] who also reported seeing the American prisoner. This is her story:

The woman she saw was white, beautiful and charming. She was not too slim, nor too fat. Her hair was red—not too short, nor too long. She had curly or wavy hair. She appeared to Ana to be in her early twenties.

She smiled and, from the place where she was staying, asked Ana to wash her clothing for her. Ana said that she would like to help her and wanted to, because she was going to be paid for it. Ana

140

spoke to the woman only at the times when the woman asked her to do the laundry for her. The beautiful clothing which was brought to her house to wash was not Japanese-made but European. They were just a few dresses, which were all marked.

She and the woman did not get into any long conversations because she was upstairs on the veranda of the hotel, which had two stories, and Ana was downstairs. The owner of the house lived up near the front, but it was operated by some Japanese. There were some house orders restricting visitors. From her house across the street, she was easily able to see the place where the prisoner was confined. The policemen were always guarding her. Even Ana was followed by policemen. When the woman left the house, it was in the car that belonged to the house where she was staying.

Ana had heard that Matilda, who lived nearby was given a ring by the woman. But Ana was not interested in knowing about it. She was fearful because she considered that the times were getting dangerous. She heard from the Japanese that they were soon going to fight against the Americans—by 1941. Ana had noticed that there was quite a bit of Japanese naval activity at the time.

Ana didn't know what the prisoner had been doing. But she had heard that she had been piloting a plane and that the Japanese had brought it to Saipan after the crash.

She never heard the woman's name mentioned or heard where she was from. Ana said she knew she was a foreigner other than a Japanese because of her looks. Even the powder she was using was not Japanese powder. The powder and lotion were of another kind.

Ana washed her clothes for one month. After that, she wasn't called over to pick up the clothes. Later she saw the woman in jail. Ana saw the woman there when she visited her brother Juan the third day he was in prison. Juan was transferred to another place then where greater punishments were given. Ana saw the woman in the place for lesser offenses. Ana looked at her several times but did not have a chance to be real close to her because she was afraid of

141

what the Japanese would do to her. She was able to see that she was combing her red hair and powdering her face. In jail the woman was wearing something like a nightgown with a low neckline. It was something like a kimono or pajama.

She saw her at least three times. When her brother was moved to the other jail, she was never allowed to enter the building. Because her brother had been transferred, Ana didn't know what happened to the woman.

Curious because of the interview questions, Ana wanted to know if they were still looking for the woman. Bendowske told her that the admiral who was on Guam was very interested in the fate of Amelia Earhart.

Jesús Salas

When Fred Goerner was on Saipan in September of 1960, he talked with Jesús Salas,[4] who had been in Garapan prison and was now a farmer. Salas was also interviewed on December 13, 1960 by Special Agent Joseph M. Patton of the navy. Manny Muña also told Buddy Brennan about Salas[5] as he showed Brennan the Garapan prison. In 1991 Muña gave me additional information about him.

The accounts given by Salas are possibly more contradictory than those of any other person that may have had contact with Amelia Earhart and Fred Noonan. When I discussed these conflicting accounts with Muña, he gave me a reasonable explanation. Other witnesses had told conflicting stories perhaps for the same reasons.

Muña had also told Brennan why the witnesses changed their stories, or were afraid to tell what they really knew. The people were afraid to say much when the CIA operation was on Saipan, because they were afraid they might lose their jobs or be put in jail—they didn't know their rights. Some were also afraid that they would arouse the anger of those who had been Japanese sympathizers on the island, who may have been responsible for the imprisonment, mistreatment and deaths of Earhart and Noonan. Those who were

142

responsible for such actions of course would have been unwilling to say what they knew for fear of being punished.

Jesús Salas

Muña said that when Salas first gave out information he was afraid to give out any more. Many people were interrogated and were told that what they were talking about was a very sensitive issue. They were talking about the Japanese executing an American woman. This information could be a national disaster for the Japanese or Americans. This is what the local people there thought during that time.

The story Salas told Goerner was that he had been put in Garapan prison in 1937 after he fought with a Japanese soldier who

143

had spit on a religious procession. He remained in prison until 1944 when American marines released him. Sometime during 1937, a white woman was placed in the next cell. She was kept there only a few hours. He saw the woman only once. His description of her fitted those given by the other witnesses. The guards told him the woman was an American pilot the Japanese had captured.

Goerner also reports that after he interviewed him Salas had told a navy investigator (probably Patton) that the Japanese had talked of taking an American woman flier prisoner in the Marshall Islands. The Japanese had bragged about capturing American fliers, a man and woman, near Jaluit in the Marshalls.

Tom Devine's book includes the special report made by Patton. The report states that on December 13, 1960, Salas said he had been a prisoner of the Japanese for many years before WW II. He is described by Patton as an illiterate Saipanese who spoke through Sheriff Sablan, who was acting as interpreter. Before WW II Salas had worked in the prison for a Japanese police sergeant by the name of Kinashi, who was killed on Saipan in 1944. Kinashi reportedly was a warden at the Garapan jail, and Salas had become his lacky.

On one occasion Salas overheard Kinashi and another Japanese talking about a white woman's airplane crashing at or near Jaluit Atoll in the Marshall Islands. He did not hear whether the pilot was picked up or what happened to her. Salas said that no white woman was ever in that prison. He would have known about it if there had been because he had the run of the entire cell blocks. Patton's note at the end of the report was that he was not sure of the reliability of Salas' testimony, but one thing that Salas had said on another matter had proven to be correct.

When Buddy Brennan visited Garapan prison with Manny Muña, Muña showed Brennan the cell in which Salas had been held. Muña told Brennan that Salas had been a farmer serving a long sentence for stealing cattle, but he escaped in 1944 when the bombing started. Brennan asked Muña when Salas last saw Earhart, and Muña answered that Salas had told many stories to many different people after his escape. Unfortunately he was no longer living to answer that question himself. Muña told Brennan that Earhart was seen in the prison as late as 1941. Muña stated that his sister, Joaquina Muña Cabrera, among others, saw Earhart when they worked in this area. After the war started, no one except the Japanese were permitted inside the prison compound. But in Muña's family it was said that the woman prisoner had been there much longer.

When I talked with Muña on Saipan in April of 1991, I asked him about the two men in jail who were imprisoned along with Amelia Earhart and Fred Noonan on Saipan. He told me that two cattle rustlers had been in prison with Amelia and Fred. Amelia was in the first cell, the two rustlers were in the two middle cells and Fred was in the fourth cell.

There were two buildings with cell blocks—this was the smaller of the two. Muña told me that the Japanese had put Earhart and Noonan in the smaller prison, because they could watch them more easily.

When I asked Muña the names of the prisoners, he said that one was Jesús Salas, but he didn't want to mention the other person's name. The man was still alive, and Muña did not want to reveal his name because he would be upset about people talking about him. He is a prosperous businessman today, and he would be embarrased if his prison record were made public. Muña didn't want to hurt the man's reputation.

It would certainly be helpful if someone could interview this surviving prisoner about Amelia Earhart and Fred Noonan, especially if no investigator has spoken with him before.

At the time Muña had learned the account which Josephine Blanco Akiyama had given to the newspaper, in 1960 Salas was working for Muña, because he was his neighbor on Muña's farm. Salas told Muña about how the two prisoners communicated with each other. They would shout to each other when the guards were not in the vicinity. Salas did not understand what they said, as he did not know English.

Muña told me that Amelia Earhart and Fred Noonan were last seen in 1944 when Salas was still in prison. He also said that Salas, during his interview with Goerner, recognized the picture of Amelia Earhart, even though he did not know her name. However, Goerner does not mention this in his book.

* * *

In October, 1991, Manny Muña sent me clippings of an article titled, "Cryptic Clues Add to Earhart Puzzle" from the September 22, 1991, issue of the Guam *Pacific Sunday News*. In it Timothy Spence wrote that Nito Blas, mayor of Manigilao, whose family lived on Saipan during World War II, said his father and uncle were used as workers at a Japanese command center near present-day Charlie Dock. The mayor said that Segundo Blas (his uncle) and Thomas L.G. Blas (his late father) saw a blindfolded American woman being led into a command post by soldiers on Saipan after her plane crashed in Tanapag Lagoon, between Charlie Dock and Managaha Island.

The article also tells about José Guitierrez of Agana Heights, Guam, who was a police officer on Guam when the island was invaded in December, 1941. He was put into prison at first, then he was pressed into service by the occupation forces as a guide. He recalled that among those working as a translator for the Japanese was Juan T. ("Bokui") Borja. Borja told Guitierrez of an American woman pilot being held captive on Saipan. Guitierrez went on to say that Borja was bragging that the Americans could not win and even had to have women pilots fighting for them.

The article continues that Guitierrez himself said that they were held on Saipan at least into the early war years. He remembered that he had met a woman in California more than a decade after the war who had taken meals to her father, a guard at the Japanese prison, and who recalled hearing stories about the American woman who was a prisoner.

146

16

Their Deaths

"I watch and they take her to this place where there is a hole been dug. They make her kneel in front then they tear the blindfold from her face and throw it into the hole. The soldiers shoot her in the chest and she fall backwards into the grave."–Nieves Cabrera Blas to Buddy Brennan.[1]

The Goerner Account

SEVERAL WITNESSES ON Saipan told Fred Goerner in the sixties about how Amelia Earhart and Fred Noonan may have died. José Pangelinan,[2] a grocery store owner, had known many of the Japanese officers before and during the war. They told him about an American man and woman who were held and later killed by the *Kempeitei*. He said that the man was executed by samurai sword the day after the woman's death. But he was not an eyewitness to the execution.

The Davidson Account

In their two visits to Saipan in 1967 and 1968, Don Kothera and his companions talked with Anna Magofna,[3] who reported that as a seven or eight-year-old, she had witnessed the beheading of a white man. She had been walking home from school when she observed two Japanese with a white woman and a white man with a long nose. The Japanese made them dig a hole. After they blindfolded the man, they made him kneel. Then, they cut off his head with a samurai sword and kicked him into the grave.

The Devine Account

In an interview appearing in the *Japan Times* on November 12, 1970, a woman from Japan offered information as to how Amelia Earhart may have died. Thomas Devine writes that Mrs. Michiko Sugita[4] claimed that Japanese military police shot her as a spy on Saipan in 1937. At the time, Sugita's father, Mikio Suzuki, was civilian chief of police at Garapan. As a girl of eleven she overheard the police describe to her father their execution of an American woman aviator. Devine comments that Mrs. Sugita's testimony was the first of a Japanese national to link the disappearance of Amelia Earhart to Japanese authorities on Saipan.

Michiko Sugita

148

Devine wrote to Michiko Sugita for further information. In a letter, apparently written on August 12, 1971, she told him of her early years in the eastern Caroline Islands where her father was chief of police. He was then promoted to district chief, and he and his family moved to Saipan. She wrote that she overheard many conversations between her father and the police, often regarding Amelia Earhart.

She also mentioned a controversial issue which had divided Saipan police in 1937. There were some who did not think the flier should be executed. They said she was a fine, beautiful person. But Mikio Suzuki said that since she had come there as a spy, she must be executed.

Devine continues that in her letters Michiko Sugita portrayed her father as a man who did only what he was ordered by the Japanese military and wrote that it was unfortunate that the police had to obey the military. Sugita also stated that she believed that Amelia Earhart was executed in Saipan.

In a letter of December 18, 1972, she wrote Devine that regardless of the circumstances, killing should not be tolerated or pardoned. She felt in a way that her father deserved an execution by poison. Of course she would be happier if he were alive, but that was all in the past.

The Loomis Account

Vincent Loomis learned from Florence Kirby and Olympio Borja[5] about how Earhart and Noonan may have died. They had been told by a farmer that he had seen two Americans, a man and a woman, near Garapan cemetery. The farmer, who was no longer alive at the time Loomis questioned Kirby and Borja, told the women that one evening he went to the back of his pasture where his cow was tethered. Just as he was approaching the cow, he saw the Japanese marching two persons toward the cemetery. The prisoners were wearing khaki uniforms and had their hands tied behind them and bags over their heads. One was taller than the other, and the skin on their arms was white. The farmer hid and stayed out of sight until almost midnight, fearing he would be killed if discovered. He believed the two were executed.

Kirby and Borja also spoke about an incident regarding a Japanese policeman before the war. One night, when he was having dinner with his thirteen-year-old daughter, he was interrupted by a number of drunken police officers who boasted of killing two Americans—a man and a woman.

The Knaggs Account

Oliver Knaggs made a brief visit to Saipan. Although he does not give the date of his visit, it was apparently in 1981. During his stay he contacted Tomas Camacho,[6] the Bishop of Saipan.

Bishop Camacho had become interested in the Earhart mystery while he was a student in a California seminary. At that time he was able to meet Josephine and Maximo Akiyama who were also living in California. The bishop put Knaggs in touch with his uncle, Gregorio Camacho,[7] a former judge and an officer of the church of San Roque, Saipan. Fred Goerner had interviewed him earlier, but the Knaggs interview is much more detailed.

Knaggs writes that Camacho seemed shocked that the investigator would question that Earhart and Noonan were ever on Saipan. Knaggs asked if they had been brought to Saipan by the Japanese, and Camacho answered yes. He then qualified his answer by saying that the Japanese told them the fliers had crashed their plane on Saipan and were in fact spies.

Knaggs wondered if the Japanese had held them prisoners, and Camacho responded that they were held in the Garapan prison. Knaggs countered that he had heard that they stayed in some sort of hotel. Camacho said no, they were held in jail. The woman was often taken to the big three-story building of the Japanese officials for questioning.

When Knaggs asked about the man, Camacho said that the man did not behave himself. The Japanese had brought him some *misu* soup, a favorite breakfast food. The man insulted them by throwing it at them. Camacho said that he was instantly beheaded— a statement that Knaggs could not believe.

Camacho insisted that the man had committed a grave insult. For a prisoner to behave in that fashion could not be tolerated. Knaggs still expressed some doubts at this, but Camacho declared that it was such a big insult, such an unheard of thing, that the Japanese had talked about it openly for weeks.

Knaggs then shifted the subject to Earhart's fate, and wondered if she had been tried as a spy. Camacho did not know, but he did know that she had been taken to a building for questioning. Knaggs said he had heard that Earhart had been brought to Saipan to be tried as a spy. They both had already been declared spies, Camacho answered. They had been paraded in front of the people who were told that they were American spies.

The Brennan Account

When Buddy Brennan visited Saipan, he spoke with some people previous investigators had not interviewed. After talking with Muña, he met a young girl named Rosa. She was the granddaughter of Muña's sister, Joaquina Muña Cabrera (who had been interviewed by Goerner).

Rosa offered to help arrange a meeting with a woman who knew a lot about Earhart. Brennan writes that it was from that casual, seemingly insignificant beginning that they were to make their major discovery.

He said that Rosa acted as guide and interpreter, taking them along a winding back road to a modest farmhouse, where they met Mrs. Nieves Cabrera Blas,[8] whom Brennan considered to be a remarkable woman with a remarkable story.

Brennan said that the woman they were soon to call Nieves was somewhat nervous with her foreign visitors. She was an elegant Chamorran with a light, unlined complexion, even though she was nearly seventy. She had a slightly built figure and looked at her visitors alertly.

151

Brennan asked her if she recalled seeing the American woman flier and the man called Fred Noonan when they were there on the island. Nieves wanted to be sure that Rosa had been correct in saying that Brennan was not from the CIA.

Rosa

Brennan said her question startled him. He assured her he was not part of that operation and said he was seeking information because Earhart's family would appreciate knowing Amelia's fate.

With that explanation of Brennan's mission, Nieves stated that when the Japanese were on Saipan, she had lived with her family on a farm near the village of Garapan. Part of their farm was next to a large fence which the Japanese had built to protect their base. When Japan was at war with the United States, her family had to have a special pass to enter the area, which was off-limits to other Saipanese.

152

Nieves said that one day, before the war, there was excitement in the village. People were saying that the Japanese had captured two spies, and were holding them in town. She went to see the prisoners in the square where the Japanese police building was. She saw them and discovered that one of the two that she had thought was a man was actually a woman. She added that the Japanese guards made the prisoners take off all their clothes after they had been brought into town.

Nieves Cabrera Blas

It was only then that she could tell that one of the two who were considered spies was a woman. She learned that the woman's name was Amelia Earhart and that she was a flier and regarded as an American spy.

What she witnessed is described, not only in Brennan's book, but also on his videotape. In addition, a dramatization of her experience in which Mrs. Blas plays herself, is given in the November 7, 1990, TV show, "Unsolved Mysteries." According to the program, Buddy Brennan's interview with Nieves had taken place in 1987.

Then she had told Brennan that she did not see either one of the two people again for many years. In the "Unsolved Mysteries" account, however, it appears that only a short time elapsed between the times she saw the man and the woman. She had heard from other people that the woman was in a little prison building but she was never brought outside the fence again.

After the war had been going on for several years the people of Saipan were surprised to be bombed by ships and airplanes. The Japanese told them it was the Americans. If they landed on their island they would all be killed—so they must go to the caves.

Nieves told Brennan that one day when she was working on her farm, she saw three Japanese motorcycles. Amelia Earhart was in a little seat on the side of one motorcycle. She was wearing handcuffs and she was blindfolded. As Nieves watched they took Amelia to a place where there was a hole that had been recently dug. They made her kneel in front of it. Then they tore the blindfold from her face and threw it into the hole. The soldiers shot her in the chest and she fell backwards into the grave.

In trying to determine the date of Amelia Earhart's death, Brennan reports that there had been a preliminary bombing a few months prior to the invasion of Saipan. Around February 1944, Admiral Marc Mitscher made a strike on Saipan. There was no attempt to land troops, however. The Japanese on Saipan were caught unprepared and panicked. However, the invasion of Saipan didn't happen until June of 1944. Word was spread even to the Japanese field troops that they were getting pushed back on all fronts. They were poorly equipped to defend Saipan.

Brennan believes that when the Japanese planned to defend Saipan, they determined that Amelia Earhart had to be executed, which would have been sometime between February and June of 1944.

17

Their Burials

"They are buried here, beneath us!"—an Okinawan woman to Thomas Devine.[1]

The Devine Account

IN 1944 AUTHOR TOM DEVINE participated in the invasion of Saipan. Then an army sergeant, he was the top non-commissioned officer of the not-yet-activated 244th Army Postal Unit commanded by First Lieutenant Fritz W. Liebig of Bismarck, North Dakota. The unit became the nucleus of the Army Garrison Force commanded by General Sanderford Jarman, which was then engaged in combat with Japanese forces in the northern sector of the island.

In mid-July 1945, he and Pfc John Boggs from Denver, Colorado, went exploring in southern Garapan. Boggs photographed some sights, and, together, they also explored a Chamorro cemetery nearby.

A few days later, Devine returned to the cemetery with other soldiers. An Okinawan woman[2] came to them. Through an interpreter she said she knew where two white people, one of whom was a woman, were buried. The woman indicated that the people had come from the sky, and then indicated with her gestures where the

155

grave was located. When Devine walked with her to the spot, the woman said that they were buried underneath them. Devine writes that there were grave markers in the Chamorro cemetery and plain crosses in the temporary graveyard, but no markers where the Okinawan woman pointed. The woman also indicated that the Japanese had killed them. Devine determined later that the site was approximately one-hundred yards north and slightly west of the Chamorro cemetery.

Devine returned to Saipan in 1963 with Fred Goerner and Goerner's associate to find the gravesite, eventually pinpointing what he states is the Earhart-Noonan grave along the western edge of the postwar road.

The Gervais Report

While on Guam Gervais interviewed two men with similar stories about the deaths and burial of the two American fliers. Ben Salas,[3] age forty-three, had been a carpenter at the Chico Navy Base in 1937 and was currently working at a lumberyard in Agana, Guam. Joaquin Seman,[4] age forty-eight, had been employed at the sugar mill on Saipan in 1937.

Both men stated that they remembered two Americans on Saipan in 1937, and that one was the American spy woman. Salas made the remark that the executions did not take place at the prison. Gervais, taken by surprise, excitedly asked if they had indeed been executed. Both agreed that the prisoners were executed at the prison on the main Chico base.

Seman said that Jesús Guerrero knew all about it. The fliers were buried after the execution. Seman and Salas offered to take Gervais to the cemetery if he wanted to go. At that time, however, Gervais was still on Guam and had not yet received permission to go to Saipan. Gervais wrote that he had a hard time accepting this information which he heard for the first time. He wanted to know if they were the same Americans whose fate he was trying to learn.

Ben Salas

Salas answered that there were only two Americans killed on Saipan before the war by the Japanese—an American man and an American woman. When Gervais asked where they were buried, Salas answered that the cemetery was located in Liang on Saipan next to the quarry near a lumberyard. It was about a mile south of the main prison that the Japanese had built before the war.

Both Salas and Seman believed that the graves were still there. Although many cemeteries had been bombed during the 1944 invasion, the one in question apparently remained intact. The specific graves could be located through the Catholic church on Saipan. The islanders said Earhart and Noonan were buried in the Catholic cemetery because the Japanese thought at the time the Americans were Catholic.

157

In hopes that there might be church records of the gravesites, the investigators visited Father Arnold Bendowske when they went to Saipan in 1960. He located records from 1924 to 1943, but there was no listing of the fliers. He said that if Noonan and Earhart were not Catholics, the graves could have been placed in unconsecreated ground adjacent to the church cemetery. But no records existed for that area.

The Goerner Accounts

During his investigations, Goerner talked with marine corps Colonel Justin Chambers,[5] who had earned a Congressional Medal of Honor and had served with the Fourth Marine Division both at Kwajalein and Saipan. While on Saipan, Chambers heard that a grave containing two American fliers, a man and woman, had been found.

Alex Rico[6] of Torrence, California had been with a Seabee outfit on Saipan in 1944 and 1945. His Seabee encampment on Saipan was located north of Tanapag Harbor on the Japanese naval seaplane base. Rico served as an interpreter with the Saipanese because he spoke Spanish. Rico told Goerner that several islanders said the Japanese had been bragging before the war of capturing some white people. They had brought them to Saipan, where they were buried near a native cemetery. There was a small native cemetery that was located within the area. There also was a native graveyard south of Garapan City. Rico felt the natives had been telling the truth.

On one of his Saipan trips, Goerner was told by grocery store owner José Pangelinan[7] that although he had not witnessed the burial, he had heard that the American fliers had been buried together in an unmarked grave outside the cemetery south of Garapan City. The actual gravesite was known only to the Japanese, who said the two were fliers and spies.

While on Saipan Goerner also met Remedios Jons,[8] whom he describes as a small, shy Chamorran woman in her mid-fifties who lived in a tiny house near San Roque Village and had responded to Goerner's plea for the help of anyone who knew of the old cemetery and its connection with two American fliers. She told Goerner that before the war a Japanese soldier had shown her and her sister the unmarked grave of an American man and woman outside the cemetery. The soldier mentioned that the man and woman had been fliers and were killed as spies. She believed the area she had been shown was outside the southeast corner of the Garapan cemetery.

The Davidson Account

In 1968 on their second trip to Saipan, Anna Magofna[9] showed the Kothera group where she believed that Amelia Earhart and Fred Noonan were buried. She was certain she could find it because she had gone by the grave every day on her way to school until the invasion destroyed Garapan. She believed that they had been cremated by the Japanese, and that the grave was outside the cemetery near a crematorium.

As the group went with her to find the grave, she said she remembered some coconut trees near the cemetery and also a large breadfruit tree. When she found the breadfruit tree, she remarked that the grave was about ten steps from the tree. The tree was an old tree—perhaps fifty or sixty years old—and very large for the area but almost dead. Since she had been hiding from the Japanese at the time of the burial, she could not tell how deep the grave was, but she thought it would not be as deep as a Chamorro grave.

The next day, the men dug where she had indicated. They believed the grave had already been excavated, but they still found some human bones and a gold bridge. Dr. Raymond S. Baby, associate professor of Anthropology at Ohio State University, examined these items a few months later. He concluded his report by saying: It is our opinion that the cremated remains are those of a female, probably white individual between the anatomical ages of forty to forty-two years. A single unburnt bone is...the remains of a second individual, male."[10]

The Brennan Account

Buddy Brennan was also shown a place where it was said that Amelia Earhart was buried. Mrs. Nieves Blas[11] told him that after she had seen Amelia Earhart executed and fall backwards into the grave, she ran from the place so that the soldiers would not see her. Later she went back to see if they had buried her, and Nieves said they had. She was sure she could find the site of the grave again, because Amelia had been buried underneath what she said was the biggest breadfruit tree on the whole island. Nieves said she had gone there often to get breadfruit. The Japanese had taken all the food they had grown on their farm so she went there to get breadfruit to eat.

In the mid-eighties, Nieves Blas made it clear that this knowledge had bothered her since Earhart's death. She said that many stories that other islanders had told were not true, and she was relieved to have told the truth to someone at last.

Brennan and Nieves Blas drove to a large parking lot containing construction equipment, surrounded by a seven-foot security fence. She pointed to a spot just inside the wire fence, and told them about the spot where she had witnessed the execution.

The breadfruit tree had been cut down when the equipment compound was built. Nieves Blas said that when she saw them cutting the tree, she made a mental note of other visual signs so that she could continue to find the location of the grave. That was the place she remembered.

She then retold the story on tape, and mimed the shooting scene, the guards firing, then Amelia toppling backwards into a grave.

Brennan talked with the yard manager about the breadfruit tree. The yard manager remembered four or five were removed at one time, including a big one, the biggest he had ever recalled seeing. At that moment Brennan was virtually standing on the spot where it had been.

On another trip to Saipan, Brennan decided to find the bones of Earhart and Noonan. His party made an excavation on the site where the breadfruit tree had been. After hours of digging, Brennan said they found a two-foot-long scrap of cloth, with the top cut straight. Brennan said he found the bottom portion was puzzling. The center segment was a uniform width of about six or eight inches. On each side, however, it had been cut in even arcs to form thin bands at the top.

Their group looked up to find Nieves and Rosa, the young woman who had led them to Nieves, watching them. Brennan writes the older woman was staring at the fragment of earth-stained fabric with a stricken expression on her face. She then passed her hand across her face and muttered something to Rosa. The young girl turned and said that Nieves believed that the cloth was the blindfold Amelia had been wearing. The soldiers had removed it and thrown it into the grave just before they shot her.

18

Conclusion: Lost Legend

I BEGAN THIS BOOK with the question, "What really happened to American's most famous aviator and her navigator near the equator in 1937?" I have tried to find authentic accounts from witnesses who could give us the answers. But which ones are right? Or, if there is some truth and some error in their testimony—how can we determine fact from fiction?

Let us look at some alternatives as proposed by many sincere researchers. One is to assume that the stories are too contradictory to be believed. Another is to assume that they are made up by people who want to be famous or obtain money or power. Or we may say that the natives from the various islands have told sophisticated investigators what they wanted to hear in order to gain their favor. Or it could be argued that there is no point in reading what the islanders have said because the answer lies solely in the mathematical calculations in air navigation or radio communications or by determining the path of a hypothetical spy mission.

If the reports of the witnesses are completely disregarded as untrustworthy, then it is possible to come up with a number of different conclusions.

● The *Electra* ran out of gas after Earhart and Noonan were unable to find Howland Island and crashed into the ocean without a trace, at some unknown spot. This is very likely the prevailing view of the American people, as well as the official view of the United

States government. It is advocated by Elgen Long and Mary Lovell,[1] among many others.

● Amelia Earhart was so exhausted from a grueling journey that she could not fly her plane properly and crashed into the ocean before reaching Howland Island. This view has been publicly expressed by Al Bresnik,[2] Earhart's personal photographer, who also thought she might have been pregnant during her round-the-world attempt.

● Earhart and Noonan had no intention of landing on Howland Island because they were on a spy mission. They continued on to the Phoenix Islands, according to a previous plan, but crashed on one of them and perished a few days later. This view has most recently been held by Richard Gillespie[3] who believed that he found evidence of the *Electra* and a shoe belonging to Amelia.

● Earhart and Noonan flew directly from Lae, New Guinea to Saipan. With this theory, the testimony of only the Marshall Islanders is completely disregarded. This view was held by Paul Briand, who was unaware of the Marshall Islands testimony. It is also held by Tom Devine.

● Earhart and Noonan flew to the Gilberts, where Earhart chose to live for the rest of her life. This theory was presented at least a couple of times in a tabloid[4] with a picture of her. A recent book[5] also states that the *Electra* was shot down over the Gilberts.

It is not my intention to argue the pros and cons of the various theories, but to argue in favor of the testimony of the witnesses as providing the most accurate picture of what really happened.

Although most of the witnesses were reluctant to tell what they knew when they weren't sure that they could trust the investigators, once this distrust was removed, they did their best to recall what they had experienced.

The difficulties involved in questioning most of the witnesses— some researchers went to virtually inaccessible islands—helped to insure that only thorough interrogation and tried and true investigative techniques were employed.

Although some people who were said to have been involved in the capture or death of Earhart and Noonan have denied the allegations, the denials have been shown to be prompted by self-interest. The inconsistencies in the testimony among witnesses who saw the same event are what would normally be expected regarding any incident, especially after a long period of time. This is also true regarding the same witness whose account may vary slightly as it is retold through the years.

Even though I have presented the cumulative testimony of far more witnesses than has any previous book, there are still unanswered questions.

How can the landing on Saipan be explained? Was there a Japanese pilot who flew them there? If so, I would like to learn of at least one witness who saw him.

Did Amelia Earhart and Fred Noonan die on Saipan? If so, how and when? Where were they buried? Have their bones been recovered? I have reported what some, but not all, witnesses have said. More evidence is needed, I believe, before a more conclusive answer can be given.

What happened to the *Electra*? If it went down in the Marshalls, was it taken or flown to Saipan? Tom Devine believes he personally witnessed the destruction of the Earhart plane on Saipan, but I would like to see more support from others regarding this before commenting further.

Let us turn then to the stories given by witnesses about whom I have written. Despite the inconsistencies, I believe it is possible to reconstruct a legend about the lost fliers based on the many tales that have been told. Unless every one of the stories was fabricated (and such deception surpasses credibility), I believe the following sequence of events may well have occurred.

The Crash

As Amelia Earhart and Fred Noonan flew in their Lockheed *Electra* from Lae, New Guinea, toward Howland Island, their plane was low on fuel. They flew into a storm near Howland Island. Realizing they would be unable to make it, they attempted to land on one of the British-held Gilbert Islands.

They were off course, however, and flew north of the Gilberts towards the Marshalls instead. The Japanese fleet was holding maneuvers in the area at that time. As the *Electra* came near the Marshalls, planes from the carrier *Akagi* were launched to force the *Electra* down. One pilot, Fujie Firmosa, saw the plane, and fired on it. The *Electra* then crashed near Mili Atoll.

The Capture on Land

The plane was observed coming down by a native fisherman, whose name was Lijon. The engines were not running as it came near the water. Then it landed on a reef about two-hundred feet from Barre Island of Mili Atoll. When it crashed, Fred Noonan injured his head, which started to bleed, and cut his knee. Amelia helped him get out of the plane and into their yellow life raft to go ashore. They had with them a metal container, which they buried in the coral sand under a kanal tree. A portion of the container was found years later.

Then Japanese soldiers came and started to question the two fliers. During the interrogation, the Japanese began to slap them, and Amelia Earhart screamed.

The Pickup by Ship

They were put on a fishing boat, which transferrred them to the Japanese ship, the *Koshu* or *Kamoi,* seven to ten days later. The ship left Jaluit, the Japanese headquarters in the Marshalls, was gone for about a week, and had then returned to Jaluit. Although the *Koshu* or *Kamoi* returned to Jaluit Harbor amidst considerable fanfare, the Japanese were at some pains to keep secret the exact nature of the ship's mission.

165

The Treatment

In Jaluit Harbor, a doctor from the navy dispensary and his assistant, Bilimon Amaran, were taken by launch to the ship. The doctor examined the two Americans. Amelia was unhurt, and so was not treated, but Fred was. The doctor asked Amaran to treat the wound on the forehead—there was a slight cut over his eye. There was a deep, infected cut over one knee about four inches wide. It was inflamed and bleeding slightly. Amaran used some tape on the knee. The head wound, which he cleaned, required only a bandage.

The Plane

The Japanese had picked up the *Electra,* which was in slings, on the stern of the ship. Its left wing was damaged. It was partially covered by a canvas tarp. Later it was put on a barge, and then towed to the nearby naval base at Emidj, Jaluit Atoll, where it was taken off the ship, dragged to a remote area, quickly fenced off and camouflaged.

The Confinement

Amelia and Fred were taken ashore from the ship at Jaluit Harbor to Jabor, where they were interrogated at the headquarters there. People were not permitted to go anywhere near the Americans. They were then placed in prison cells in Jaluit. A Frenchman, who was a fellow prisoner and who found out who they were, later wrote a message in a bottle saying that Amelia and Fred were prisoners in Jaluit. He threw the bottle overboard off the Spanish coast, and it was found on a French beach in October 1938.

Kwajalein

After the Americans were detained in Jaluit, they went to Kwajalein—the area naval headquarters for the Japanese. They were taken to Roi and Namor—both major Japanese bases in the Marshalls. On the island of Namor, they were taken to the military barracks where Amelia was kept in a room that was prepared for a woman, with a dresser in it. She left behind on Kwajalein a suitcase with some woman's clothing in it, a number of clippings of articles about herself, and her personal diary.

Saipan Landing

Amelia and Fred were taken by a Japanese plane from the Marshalls to Saipan. As the plane descended towards Tanapag Harbor, it hit the tops of some iron trees in the coffee plantation near the beach. The plane went on for a short distance and then crash-landed on the beach about two to three thousand feet from the main Japanese Chico Naval Base at Tanapag Village. There were Japanese Navy personnel and other non-Japanese construction workers in the area of the crash.

Saipan Capture

Some navy *Kiogan* officers soon arrived, (some carrying swords), as well as soldiers. The Americans were held under guard at the dock area until a Japanese military car arrived from Garapan, just south of Tanapag Harbor. They were blindfolded, and stripped, and then taken to the military police headquarters and interrogated for several hours. A man named Gregorio Sablan served as interpreter. Amelia was taken to Garapan prison and Fred to Muchot Point military police barracks.

Saipan Hotel

After being held in prison for only a few hours, Amelia was taken to the Kobayashi Royokan Hotel, which the military police had taken over in the mid-thirties to house political prisoners. Her papers were put in a briefcase and into a safe.

While she was at the hotel, two women, Joaquina Muña Cabrera, and Ana Villagomez Benevente, were given her clothes to clean. Each day Amelia came out into the yard of the hotel and walked around it.

167

She was watched at the hotel by detectives daily, keeping her from coming and going as she wished. She was probably hurt by the police, for she had bruises, and was seen holding her arm close to one side. Her neck appeared to have burn marks on the right side. Her left forearm was bandaged. She used an outdoor toilet, and while going to and from it, she became acquainted with a family in a house next to the hotel.

One day when Amelia was visiting this family, she sat down next to a young girl named Matilda, who was doing geography homework about the islands of the Marianas and the rest of Micronesia. As the young girl was writing on the map, Amelia took the pencil and the book from her and pointed out the island near which her plane went down.

Matilda's family offered Amelia some broiled breadfruit, and she ate a little. The family also offered fresh fruit from the kitchen. She took some fruit but then had to go back to the hotel.

On another occasion, Amelia gave Matilda's sister, Consolacion, a ring from her finger and put her hand on the girl's hand in friendship. The ring held a single pearl in a white gold setting.

Saipan Prison
Amelia had a problem with diarrhea or dysentery; the Japanese at the hotel said she died of it. Despite her illness, she was transferred to the Garapan prison, where Fred was. Both were permitted to exercise out in the main prison yard for short times during the day.

At first they had difficulty eating prison food. They were fed small portions three times a day of a diet which included breadfruit and soup.

Amelia and Fred were in a cell block of only four cells. Amelia was in cell No.1, Jesús Salas, who had been imprisoned as a teenager for cattle rustling was in cell No. 2, another cattle rustler in cell No. 3, and Fred in cell No. 4.

Their Deaths

One day the the Japanese brought Fred Noonan some *misu* soup, a favorite Japanese breakfast food. But he threw it back at the guards and was instantly beheaded.

Eventually, Amelia was taken out of the prison. She was placed in a sidecar of a motorcycle, was handcuffed and blindfolded, taken to a place where a hole had been dug and made to kneel in front of it. The guards tore the blindfold from her face and threw it into the hole. The soldiers then shot her in the chest and Amelia fell backwards into the grave.

Their Graves

Amelia and Fred were buried in a temporary cemetery, not one of the established ones. Their grave may have been one-hundred yards north and slightly west of the Chamorro cemetery near Garapan, perhaps near a very large breadfruit tree. It has also been identified as in a cemetery located in Liang on Saipan next to a quarry and lumberyard—about a mile south of the main Japanese prison. The grave was unmarked.

Final Words

The legend which I have told is no doubt partially true and partially fiction. That is the nature of a legend. Perhaps more information will come to light which can make the story more accurate.

But in my opinion it is most likely that Amelia and Fred did survive after their plane went down, that they were captured by the Japanese and eventually imprisoned on Saipan.

It is not a pretty story. It has a tragic ending. The tragedy is even greater if it is not known or ignored. But if something of what I have described really did happen, then Amelia and Fred would have wanted their fate to be known, especially to Americans.

If this book has revealed something of the true legend of the lost Amelia Earhart and Fred Noonan, then it will have accomplished its purpose.

169

Appendix 1

What Eyewitnesses Said in Their Own Words

The Year

"Somewhere around in **1937**....we saw a man....and there was a female with him." Bilimon Amaran, c. 1979, Loomis, p. 107.

"In the summer of **1937** I saw the girl twice." Antonio M. Cepada, 1960, Klaas, p. 81.

"In **1937**....I saw the American girl." Matilda Fausto Arriola, 1960, Klaas, p. 120.

"[It was **1937**] because that was the year I graduated from Japanese school. I was eleven years old that year." Josephine Blanco Akiyama, 1960, Goerner, p. 3.

"I was twenty-five or twenty-six. It was **1937 or 1938**." Joaquina Muña Cabrera, 1962, Goerner, p. 239.

The Plane

"I saw this **airplane** and the woman pilot and the Japanese taking the woman and the man with her away. [I saw it] over there...next to Barre Island. That's where it landed." Clement's wife, 1979, Loomis, p. 89.

"I was surprised to see the **airplane** hanging at the back side of the ship. The left wing was broken." Amaran, 1980s, Brennan, p. 104.

"As we stood there...the ship was towing a barge. On the barge was an **airplane**. It was partially covered but I could tell it was silver-colored. It was smaller than, and did not resemble, the Japanese seaplanes we were familiar with....it had two props. I could not see the tail." John Heine, 1980s, Brennan, p. 89.

The Capture

"The military surrounded the pilot standing up and pushed him back away from the other person on the ground. The standing pilot tried to resist being pushed, and was knocked down by a soldier with a gun that had a bayonet on the end. While the pilot was on his back, **the soldier stood over him with a bayonet** close to his chest so he could not get up...The Japanese took all the clothes off both Americano pilots and then found out one pilot was an American girl." Thomas Blas, 1960, Klaas, p. 86.

"I saw two Americans in the back of a three-wheeled vehicle. **Their hands were bound behind them,** and they were blindfolded. One of them was an American woman." Cabrera, 1960, Klaas, p. 118.

"I saw them in the square where the Japanese building was. The **Japanese guards** made them take off all the clothes, everything they had on their bodies." Nieves Cabrera Blas, 1980s, Brennan, p. 126.

Their Nationality

"The Japanese told me they were **Americans**." Amaran, 1979, Knaggs, p. 53.

"They were ...an **American** man and an **American** woman." Ben Salas, 1960, Klaas, p. 89.

"She was an **American**." Benavente, 1977, Knaggs, p. 162.

"I saw an **American** girl who was referred to by some as the '**American** spy woman.'" Antonio M. Cepada, 1960, Klaas, p. 81.

"I heard that [she] was an **American** spy girl." Carlos Palacious, 1960, Klaas, pp. 83-84.

"I saw Jesús Guerrero, the number one insular police detective, and other Japanese escorting an **American** woman to the main base." Pedro M. Cepeda, 1960, Klaas, p. 88.

"We learn...she was a flier and an **American** spy." Nieves Cabrera Blas, 1980s, Brennan, p. 127.

"She said something in English which I did not understand. My mother knew English. My mother said she was an **American**." Arriola, 1977, Knaggs, pp. 147, 149, 151.

The Man: General Description

"He had **dark hair and blue eyes**. I remember the eyes in particular as they were of a very different color from the eyes of the Marshallese." Amaran, 1979. Knaggs, p. 63 and Loomis, 1979, p. 109.

"He was **not** what I would call **a big man**. Maybe **a little taller than me but not as thick**." Amaran, 1979, Knaggs, p. 63.

"I did not see him well because of the **bandages. He was thin and tall**." Cabrera, 1962, Goerner, p. 240.

His Injuries

"**He was cut on the head and had a gash on the knee.....**The head wound required only a bandage." Amaran, 1979, Knaggs, pp. 52, 53.

"He told me to go ahead and treat the man; **he had a little small cut on the front of his face and his knee**. I put some tape on the wounds." Amaran, 1980s, Brennan, p. 104.

"**The man...had his head hurt** in some way." Akiyama, 1960, Goerner, p. 3.

"The man seemed to be **hurt and had a bandage** on his head." Nieves Cabrera Blas, 1980s, Brennan, p. 127.

"**The man['s] head was hurt and covered with a bandage, and he sometimes needed help to move.**" Cabrera, 1962, Goerner, p. 239.

The Woman: General Description

"She was **thin**." Arriola, 1960, Klaas, p. 120.

"They were both **thin**." Akiyama, 1960, Goerner, p. 3.

"The lady was **thin**. She was **tall for a woman**." Cabrera, 1962, Goerner, p. 239.

"She was **thin, about average height**." Cepeda, 1960, Klaas, p. 83.

"[She was] **a slim girl...not fat...not big in the chest.**" Palacious, 1960, Klaas, p. 83.

"She was **average height** American girl—**not short, not extra tall**—**had thin build. Chest somewhat flat.**" Cepada, 1960, Klaas, p. 82.

Her Age

"She could have been in her **twenties**." Ana Villagomez Benavente, 1977, Knaggs, p. 160.

"[She] appeared to be about **thirty** years of age." Cepeda, 1960, Klaas, p. 89.

"[She] was maybe **thirty-five** years old." Cepada, 1960, Klaas, p. 84.

"[She was] maybe **thirty-five to thirty-six**." Palacious, 1960, Klaas, p. 84.

"I think she was a **little over thirty-eight**." Amaran, c. 1979, Loomis, p. 108.

Her Injuries

"She had **bandages on her left forearm. Also bruises or burns on the right side of her neck**." Arriola, 1960, Klaas, p. 120.

"There was on **one side of her body** something that looked like **burns** from cooking by oil. **Her hand had burn marks**." Arriola, 1977, Knaggs, p. 148.

"I think the **police** sometimes **hurt her. She had bruises** and one time **her arm was hurt**." Cabrera, 1962, Goerner, p. 239.

Her Hair

"She [had] **short hair, like a man's**." Arriola, 1960, Klaas, p. 120.

"The woman had **short-cut hair like a man**." Akiyama, 1960, Goerner, p. 3.

"Her **hair** was **short like a man's**." Cabrera, 1962, Goerner, p. 239.

"She had a **man's type haircut**." Cepeda, 1960, Klaas, pp. 88-89.

"The American woman had her **hair cut short** just **like the other pilot**. Thomas ("Buko") Blas, 1960, Klaas, p. 86.

"...with **short, blonde hair**." Amaran, 1979, Knaggs, p. 52.

"It looked **brunette** to me. It **wasn't long**. It seemed to me **like** it was **a man's hair cut, a little longer**." Arriola, 1977, Knaggs, p. 150.

"Her hair appeared to be **reddish-brown color** and **cut short like man's hair, trimmed close in the back like man**." Cepada, 1960, Klaas, p. 82.

"The girl had **short dark reddish-brown hair, cut like a man's hair in back.**" Palacious, 1960, Klaas, p. 83.

"Her **hair was red. Not too short, not too long.** She had **curly or wavy hair...not exactly a man's haircut.**" Benavente, 1977, Knaggs, pp. 156, 160.

Her Clothes

"[She was] **wearing trousers like a man.**" Amaran, 1979, Knaggs, p. 52.

"She was **dressed like a man.**" Akiyama, 1960, Goerner, p. 3.

"She **looked like a man wearing pants, a black shirt and scarf, and a leather jacket.**" Cepeda, 1960, Klaas, p. 88.

"She **wore a long-sleeved black shirt** under her flying suit which they took off." Thomas Blas, 1960, Klaas, p. 86.

"**Both of them were wearing trousers** and I had believed both were men. I had never known before a woman who wore men's trousers." Nieves Cabrera Blas, 1980s, Brennan, pp. 126-127.

"She had on what looked to me **like a man's white shirt with short sleeves...open collar.**" Palacious, 1960, Klaas, p. 86.

"She wore unusual clothes...a **long raincoat belted in the center. The color was a faded khaki.**" Cepada, 1960, Klaas, p. 82.

"The lady **wore a man's clothes** when she first came. I was given her clothes to clean. I remember **pants and a jacket.** It was **leather or heavy cloth.**" Cabrera, 1962, Goerner, p. 239.

"When I first saw her, she was wearing **man's clothes,** but later they gave her **woman's dress.**" Arriola, 1961. Goerner, p. 100.

"She asked me from the place where she was staying to wash her clothing for her. I washed her clothes for one month. **The clothing was not Japanese-made.**" Benavente, 1977, Knaggs, pp. 156-157.

"It was something like a **nightgown. Had a low neckline.**" Benavente, 1977, Knaggs, p. 163.

"She was wearing something like a **nightgown,** something that was **long.**" Arriola, 1977, Knaggs, p. 150.

Her Hotel

"In 1937 an American girl stayed at the military-operated **Hotel Kobayashi Royokan**....I saw the American girl in the hotel." Arriola, 1977, Klaas, p. 120.

"I did laundry for the prisoner who stayed [at the **Kobayashi Royokan Hotel.**] Cabrera, 1962, Goerner, p. 239.

"She was quartered on the second floor of the **Hotel Kobayashi Royokan** in the summer of 1937. I saw the girl twice on two separate occasions outside the hotel over a period of two or three months." Cepada. 1960, Klaas, p. 81.

"She was upstairs on the veranda...at this house or **hotel.** We were on the north and they were on the south side of the street." Benavente, 1977, Knaggs, pp. 156-157.

"The first time I saw her was at a window on the second floor of the **hotel.**" Palacious, 1960, Klaas, p. 83.

Her Name

"I heard her name at the time. The Japanese...call her **"Amee'la, Amee'la, Amee'la."** Amaran, 1980s, Brennan, p. 104.

"We learn in the village the woman's name is: **AMELIA EARHART.**" Nieves Cabrera Blas, 1980s, Brennan, p. 127.

177

Appendix 2

IDENTIFICATION OF NAMES

Note: AE=Amelia Earhart FN=Fred Noonan
WWII=World War II

ADA, JOSÉ. Interviewed by Gervais on Guam about AE being on Saipan.

ADA, JUAN. Native judge under Japanese—said did not know AE on Saipan.

AJIMA. Japanese trader who said American woman flier's plane crashed near Jaluit.

AKIYAMA, JOSEPHINE BLANCO. Saw two white people on Saipan in 1937.

AKIYAMA, MAXIMO. Josephine's husband. With Goerner to Saipan in 1960.

ALDAN, MANUEL. Saipan dentist. Heard about captured fliers from patients.

ALIBAR, JORORO. Showed Loomis on map crash site of *Electra* on Mili Atoll.

AMARAN, BILIMON. Treated FN for injuries in Jaluit, Marshalls.

AQUININGO, MRS. JUANA. Former Saipan resident. Interviewed by Gervais.

ARRIOLA, MATILDA FAUSTO. Saw AE next door, recognized AE photo.

BABY, DR. RAYMOND S. Anthropologist who examined remains found on Saipan.

BARRAT, GENEVIEVE. Found bottle message in 1938 in France about AE-FN.

BARRE ISLAND NATIVES. Told Loomis of seeing aircraft shot down.

BASA, JOSÉ. Saw AE-FN Saipan landing, their arrest, and blind-folding.

BENAVENTE, ANA VILLAGOMEZ. Washed AE's clothes. Saw her later in jail.

BENDOWSKE, FR. ARNOLD. Saipan Catholic priest. Interviewed AE witnesses.

BENIVENTE, MAYOR. Saipan mayor who initiated AE investigation on Guam.

BIKI. Native of Likiep who knew of pre-WW II plane crash in Marshalls.

BLANCO, ANTONIA. Said daughter told her of seeing two Americans in 1937.

BLAS, NIEVES CABRERA. Witnessed Amelia's death, saw burial site.

BLAS, NITO. Mayor who said father and uncle knew of AE.

BLAS, SEGUNDO. Saw AE blindfolded on Saipan after plane crashed.

BLAS, THOMAS L. G. Saw AE blindfolded on Saipan after plane crashed.

BOGAN, LT. EUGENE. On Marshalls in 1944. Elieu told him of *Electra* crash.

BOGGS, PFC JOHN. Took pictures with Devine in Garapan cemetery in 1945.

BORA, MRS. Eldest sister of Josephine Akiyama. Heard her story in 1937.

BORJA, JUAN T. "BOKUI." Translator for Japanese. Said AE captive.

BORJA, OLYMPIA. Said farmer had seen two U.S. prisoners on pre-war Saipan.

BOYCE, RICHARD F. U.S. consul in Japan learned of Japanese naval actions.

BOYER, JESÚS. Saipan farmer. Remembered AE's short hair.

BRENNAN, T.C. ("BUDDY"). Wrote *Witness to the Execution.*

BRENNAN, T.C., III. Lawyer son of "Buddy" Brennan—with him on Pacific trip.

BRESNIK, AL. Amelia Earhart's personal photographer.

BRIAND, CAPTAIN PAUL L., JR. Wrote *Daughter of the Sky.*

BRIDWELL, COMMANDER PAUL W. Saipan administrator.

BUNITAK, KUBANG. Marshallese native said AE & FN shot down near Mili.

BUSH, GEORGE. When vice president visited Saipan, Manny Muña met him.

CABRERA, ANTONIO. Had lived at Hotel Kobayashi Royokan. AE witness.

CABRERA, JOAQUINA MUÑA. Did AE's laundry. Saw AE at hotel and prison.

CABRERA, RAMON. Saw AE-FN blindfolded on Saipan. Noticed FN's whiskers.

CAMACHO, E.M. Guam detective sergeant who assisted in AE investigations.

CAMACHO, GREGORIO. Saipan farmer, saw AE-FN on Saipan.

CAMACHO, JOSÉ RIOS. AE witness now living in Los Angeles.

CAMACHO, THOMAS. Bishop of Saipan who helped Knaggs.

CAPELLI, EDARD AND BONJO. Knew of pre-WW II plane crash in Marshalls.

CARMICHAEL, HOAGY. Composer of song, "Star Dust," which was played nightly on Saipan.

CARROLL, REAR ADMIRAL KENT J. Requested Saipanese interviews.

CEPADA, ANTONIO M. Saw AE on Saipan near Kobayashi Royokan Hotel.

CEPEDA, PEDRO M. Former Saipan resident who saw AE-FN Saipan landing.

CHAMBERS, COLONEL JUSTIN. Heard on Saipan about AE-FN grave.

"CLEMENT." Navigator for Loomis group in Marshalls. His wife a key witness.

"CLEMENT'S WIFE." Saw *Electra* crash and AE-FN captured by Japanese.

CONOVER, FATHER SYLVAN. Interviewed witnesses about AE, FN on Saipan.

CONSOLACION. Sister of Matilda Fausto Arriola. Received ring from AE.

CRUZ, JOE. Saipan legislator who told Gervais about AE investigation.

CRUZ, MARIA ROBERTA DELA. Heard that AE put on map where she crashed.

DALY, RICHARD. Assisted Tom Devine in writing of his book.

DAVIDSON, JOE. Author of *Amelia Earhart Returns From Saipan.*

DAY, LINN. Wrote about Josephine Akiyama on Saipan in *San Mateo Times.*

DE BISSCHOP, ERIC. Frenchman arrested in Jaluit in 1938.

DE BRUM, OSCAR ("TONY"). His father told him of AE's capture in 1937.

DE CARIE, MARGO. AE's personal secretary. May have sent letter to her.

DEVINE, THOMAS. Wrote *Eyewitness: The Amelia Earhart Incident.*

DÍAZ, ANTONIO. Had heard of AE-FN Saipan landing when at Chico Navy Base.

DÍAZ, CONCEPCION ("CHANDE"). Owned Kobayashi Royokan Hotel. Knew of AE.

DIKLAN, QUEEN BOSKET. Had heard about crash of *Electra* at Mili Atoll.

DINGER, CAPTAIN ROBERT S. Went with Joe Gervais for Guam investigations.

DOMINIC, GIDEON. Found container buried by AE and FN under a kanal tree.

EARHART, AMELIA. Pilot of *Electra* in unsuccessful flight around the world.

ELLIS, CAPTAIN. U.S. Marine Corps spy in the Pacific—killed by the Japanese.

ETHELL, JEFFREY. Co-author with Loomis of *Amelia Earhart: The Final Story*.

FAUSTO, JOSEPA DÍAZ. Mother of Matilda Fausto (San Nicholas) Arriola.

FELIPE. Talked with AE on Saipan. Brother of Matilda Fausto Arriola.

FIORILLO, MARTY. Accompanied Don Kothera on his second trip to Saipan.

FIRMOSA, FUJIE. Japanese pilot from the Carrier *Akagi* who shot down AE's plane.

FLORES, BISHOP. Translated interviews of Fr. Bendowske's Saipan witnesses.

FORD, GERALD R. U.S. president who signed Saipan covenant in 1976.

FUCHIDA, CAPTAIN MITSUO. Japanese pilot who led Pearl Harbor attack from the carrier *Akagi*.

GACEK, JOHN. Accompanied Don Kothera on his late 1960s trips to Saipan.

"GALVAN," VICENTE. Denied then later admitted knowledge of AE on Saipan.

GEREYO, JOSÉ. Witness who told Brother Gregorio of AE-FN Saipan landing.

GERVAIS, MAJOR JOE. U.S. Air Force officer who began AE investigations in 1960.

GESECHKE, JACK, Accompanied Don Kothera on his second trip to Saipan.

GILLESPIE, RICHARD. Believes AE-FN crashed on Nikumaroro Island.

GOERNER, FRED. Author of *The Search for Amelia Earhart,* published in 1966.

GREEN, "DOC." WW II veteran who learned from Marshallese about AE-FN.

GREGORIO, BROTHER. Was told of AE-FN on Saipan by Sanchez brothers.

GUERRERO, JESÚS. Head of Saipan police during Japanese administration.

GUITIERREZ, JOSÉ. Juan T. Borja told him of AE captive on Saipan after 1941.

HASSE, WARREN. Told Goerner that Jackson found AE's diary in Marshalls.

HATFIELD, MR. Marshallese interviewed by Prymak and Gervais about AE.

HAUPTMANN, BRUNO R. Man convicted of kidnapping the Lindbergh baby.

HEINIE, CARL. Jaluit missionary who wrote about letter to AE before war.

HEINIE, DWIGHT. Marshallese who said AE's plane might have been shot down.

HEINIE, JOHN. Saw *Electra* on barge in Jaluit Harbor in 1937.

HOLLEY, CLYDE E. AE's lawyer who knew Josephine Akiyama's story.

IGATOL, LOUIS. Saw AE on Saipan in car with Japanese admiral.

JACK, LOTAN. Told Brennan AE plane was shot down in Marshalls.

JACKSON, W.B. With marines in Marshalls, found AE's diary, other items.

JAJOCK. Native of Likiep who knew of pre-WW II plane crash in Marshalls.

JARMAN, GEN. SANDERFORD. Commander of U.S. Army Garrison Force on Saipan.

JIBAMBAM, ELIEU. Told several authors that Ajima told him of AE.

JOHN, DR. Marshallese native who was shown AE & FN prison on Saipan.

JONS, REMEDIOS. Had been shown unmarked grave of AE-FN on Saipan.

KABUA, AMATA. Marshallese who believed AE had come down in Marshalls.

KABUA, KABUA. Was told that *Electra* ran out of gas, came down near Mili.

KABUA THE GREAT. The first king of the Marshall Islands.

KANNA, RALPH. Met prisoner who had AE's picture. Believed AE was executed.

KELLEHER, J.F. Learned of AE-FN plane crash in Marshalls before WWII.

KENNEDY, JOHN F. President of U.S. who terminated CIA operation on Saipan.

KINASHI, POLICE SERGEANT. Salas heard him talk about AE's Marshalls crash.

KINLEY, ROBERT. Saipan Marine found photo in 1944 of AE and Japanese.

KIRBY, FLORENCE. Said farmer saw AE-FN as prisoners on Saipan pre-WWII.

KLAAS, JOE. Author of *Amelia Earhart Lives,* about Gervais' investigations.

KNAGGS, OLIVER. Author of *Amelia Earhart: Her Last Flight*

KOTHERA, DON. Made two trips to Saipan to find *Electra* and AE-FN grave.

LEE, MR. Marshallese who met Japanese pilot who said he shot down *Electra.*

LIEBIG, 1ST LT. FRITZ. Commanding officer of Tom Devine's unit on Saipan.

LIJON. Saw *Electra* crash land near Barre Island, and capture of AE-FN.

LINDBERGH, CHARLES A. First pilot to make solo crossing of Atlantic Ocean.

LODEESEEN, CAPTAIN MARIUS. Had worked with FN at Pan Am.

LONG, ELGEN. Believes AE-FN crashed in ocean NW of Howland Islands.

LOOMIS, GEORGIE. Went with her husband to Marshall Islands in 1978.

LOOMIS, VINCENT. Author of *Amelia Earhart: The Final Story.*

LOROK. Owner of Barre Island. Lijon told him of AE-FN crash landing there.

LOVELL, MARY. Wrote *The Sound of Wings: The Life of Amelia Earhart.*

MAGHOKIAN, VICTOR. Saw discovery of AE's diary, personal belongings.

MAGOFNA, ANNA. As a seven-year-old saw a white man beheaded.

MAHAN, JOHN. Was in Marshalls in 1944. Learned of AE's crash landing there.

MATONIS, KEN. Accompanied Kothera on his late 1960s trips to Saipan.

MATSUMOTO, JOSÉ Y. Josephine Akiyama's brother-in-law. Saw AE-FN.

MAYAZO, TOMAKI. Loaded coal on ship *Kamoi* or *Koshu* which picked up AE-FN.

MAYBERRY, MR. Worked for CIA on Saipan. Showed Muña clipping about AE.

MEJIN. Gave Loomis location of metal box buried by AE-FN.

MIDDLE, RALPH. Talked with Marshallese about AE-FN who crashed pre-WWII.

MILLER, RUDOLPH. Interpreter. Learned that AE-FN had been on Kwajalein.

MITSCHER, ADMIRAL MARC. Bombed Saipan between February and June 1944.

MUÑA, MANUEL D. Talked with pilot who shot down AE's plane.

NIMITZ, ADMIRAL CHESTER W. Said AE-FN crashed, captured in Marshalls.

NOONAN, FRED. Navigator with AE on unsuccessful round-the-world flight.

OHASI, MARIA. Witness mentioned by Goerner and Devine. Known to Muña.

OKINAWAN WOMAN. Showed Devine on Saipan in 1945 grave of AE-FN.

PALACIOUS, CARLOS. Saw AE on Saipan at Kobayashi Royokan Hotel.

PANGELINAN, JOSÉ. Told Goerner of death of AE-FN on Saipan.

PARKER, ALFRED. Norwegian captain who saw 1937 naval activity at Jaluit.

PATTON, JOSEPH M. Special agent who said AE may have been on Saipan.

PENALUNA, WILLIAM. Josephine Akiyama's attorney. Urged her to tell story.

POST, WILEY. Crashed with Will Rogers in plane in 1935.

PRYMAK, BILL. President of Amelia Earhart Society of Researchers.

PUTNAM, GEORGE. Husband of Amelia Earhart. Promoter for her flights.

QUINTANILLA, JOSÉ. Guam police chief. Interviewed Saipan witnesses.

RAFFORD, JR., PAUL L. Radio expert—has studied AE's final messages.

REINECK, COL. ROLLIN C. Chief navigator of B-29s on Saipan in WW II.

REYES, JUAN. Witness mentioned by Goerner and Devine. Muña: now dead.

RICO, ALEX. Saipan natives said Japanese had bragged of taking white people.

RIOS, JESÚS. Witness who told Brother Gregorio of AE-FN Saipan landing.

ROGERS, WILL. Crashed in airplane with Wiley Post in 1935.

ROOSEVELT, FRANKLIN. President who ordered massive rescue effort for AE.

"ROSA." Joaquina Cabrera's granddaughter. Introduced Brennan to eyewitness.

SABLAN, ELIAS. Former mayor of Saipan. Held AE investigation on Guam.

SABLAN, GREGORIO. Interpreter on Saipan during AE-FN initial questioning.

SABLAN, JOSEPA REYES. Saw AE-FN taken to police headquarters, Saipan.

SABLAN, MANUEL "DEDA." First denied—later admitted seeing AE.

SABLAN, OSWALD. Worked under Japanese. Said did not know AE on Saipan.

SABLAN, SHERIFF MANUEL. Assisted Gervais in Saipan interviews.

SAKISAG, PEDRO. Witness mentioned by Goerner and Devine.

SALAS, BEN. Had been carpenter on Saipan in 1937. Believed AE executed.

SALAS, JESÚS. Saw AE in prison cell in Garapan jail, Saipan next to him.

SANCHEZ, JOSÉ AND JUAN. Told Father Gregorio of AE-FN on Saipan in 1930s.

SEMAN, JOAQUIN. Worked at Saipan sugar mill, 1937. Believed AE executed.

SHEFT, CASIMIR, DR. U.S. Navy dentist on Saipan. Mrs. Akiyama worked for him.

SLADE, JIM. WMAL commentator who recorded interview with Amaran.

SPENCE, TIMOTHY. Wrote article on AE-FN in (Guam) *Pacific Sunday News.*

STEIGMANN, JEROME P. AE researcher since 1944, ex-marine, detective.

SUGITA, MICHIKO. Daughter of Garapan police chief said AE shot in 1937.

SUSUKI, MIKIO. Garapan chief of police, Saipan in 1937. Father of Sugita.

TAKINAMI. Japanese husband of Bosket Diklan, Mili Queen.

TARDIO, FATHER. Saipan priest. Hoped Josephine Blanco would become a nun.

"TOKYO." Japanese native of Emidj, Jaluit. Saw *Electra* unloaded from barge.

"TOKYO ROSA." Name given to AE while she was on Saipan.

TRINIDAD. Matilda Fausto Arriola's niece, lost borrowed ring given by AE.

TUDELA, FRANCISCO. Witness mentioned by Goerner, Devine, and Muña.

VILLA-GOMEZ, JUAN. Was in Garapan jail same time as AE.

WABOL, MECARIA. Saw plane land in Saipan with AE-FN. FN's head bandaged.

WALLACK, ROBERT. Found briefcase on Saipan in 1944 with Earhart papers.

WILES, ERNEST E. On Tinian in 1946. Enlisted man told him of AE on Saipan.

Appendix 3

IDENTIFICATION OF PLACES

Note: AE=Amelia Earhart FN=Fred Noonan

AGANA. The capital of the U.S. Territory of Guam.

AILINGLAPALAP. A Marshall Island, near which *Electra* went down.

BARRE ISLAND. Part of Mili Atoll, Marshalls. *Electra* crash seen from there.

BOKONARIOWA ISLAND. Part of Mili Atoll, Marshalls, next to Barre Island.

CAPE HORN. A cape at the southern tip of South America.

CAROLINE ISLANDS. Group of islands in Central Pacific near Marshalls.

CHALAN KANOA. Village on Saipan on western shore south of Garapan.

CHARLIE DOCK. Name given to dock at Tanapag Harbor, Saipan.

CHICO NAVAL BASE. Next to Tanapag Harbor, Saipan.

EJOWA. Part of Mili Atoll, Marshalls, where Jororo Alibar was interviewed.

EMIDJ. Former Japanese naval base on Jaluit, to which *Electra* was taken.

FLORES POINT. Location of Chico Naval Base, Tanapag Harbor, Saipan.

GARAPAN. Largest village on Saipan. AE-FN imprisoned in jail there.

GILBERT ISLANDS. Under British control in World War II. South of Marshalls.

GUAM. An island belonging to U.S. one-hundred-twenty miles south of Saipan.

HIROSHIMA. Japanese city on which first atomic bomb was dropped.

HOWLAND ISLAND. Central Pacific island. Unreached destination of *Electra*.

JABOR. Town by Jaluit Harbor, Jaluit Atoll, Marshall Islands.

JALUIT. A Marshall Island where FN was treated by Bilimon Amaran.

KWAJALEIN. A Marshall Island on which the diary of AE was found.

LAE, NEW GUINEA. Final takeoff place of *Electra*, July, 1937.

LAULU. Part of Saipan, south of Tanapag Harbor.

LIANG. Place where a cemetery is located on Saipan.

LIKIEP ATOLL. One of the Marshall Islands.

MADAGASCAR. An island off the east coast of Africa.

MAJURO. One of the Marshall Islands, near which *Electra* went down.

MAKIN ISLAND. One of the Gilbert Islands, in the central Pacific.

MALOELAP ISLAND. A Marshall island. Letter for AE addressed there.

MANAGAHA ISLAND. Small island off the western shore of Saipan.

MANGILAO, GUAM. A community on the east coast of Guam.

MARIANAS. Chain of islands in western Pacific including Saipan and Tinian.

MARSHALL ISLANDS. Islands in central Pacific, including Mili and Jaluit.

MICRONESIA. The name for a number of small islands in the Pacific Ocean.

MILI ATOLL. A Marshall Islands atoll where the *Electra* crashed.

MUCHOT POINT. Located on western shore of Saipan, next to Garapan.

NAGASAKI. Japanese city on which second atomic bomb was dropped.

NAMUR. Also spelled Namor. See Roi Namor.

NIKUMARORO. One of the Phoenix Islands. Gillespie says AE-FN crashed there.

OKINAWA. Large Japanese island in western Pacific.

PALAU. Western Pacific island under Japanese control in World War II.

PHOENIX ISLANDS. A group of islands southwest of Howland Island.

PONAPE. An island in the central Pacific.

RATAK GROUP. Group of the Marshall Islands, including Mili and Majuro.

ROI NAMOR. Former Japanese naval base on Kwajalein in the Marshalls.

ROTA. One of the Marianas Islands.

SAIPAN. Western Pacific island in Marianas, where AE-FN held.

SAN ROQUE. Village on western shore of Saipan north of Garapan.

TAGPACHOU, MT. Highest mountain in the island of Saipan.

TANAPAG HARBOR. Harbor in Saipan where AE-FN landed in Japanese plane.

TANAPAG VILLAGE. Next to Tanapag Harbor, Saipan.

TINIAN. One of the Marianas islands, five miles south of Saipan.

TRUK. Western Pacific island under Japanese control in World War II.

YAP. Western Pacific island under Japanese control in World War II.

Notes

Preface

1. *Webster's New International Dictionary of the English Language, Second Edition, unabridged,* p. 1412.

1. First Report of the Survival

1. Knaggs, *Amelia Earhart: Her Last Flight,* p. 100.
2. Goerner, *The Search for Amelia Earhart,* pp. 163, 166.
3. Ibid., pp. 163, 166.
4. Ibid., pp. 164-166.
5. Loomis, *Amelia Earhart: The Final Story,* pp. 85-86.
6. Knaggs, *Amelia Earhart: Her Last Flight,* pp. 98, 100-101.
7. Brennan, *Witness to the Execution,* pp. 80-82 and videotape: *Witness to the Execution, the Odyssey of Amelia Earhart.*

2. Japanese Pickup at Mili Atoll

1. Knaggs, *Last Flight,* p. 56.
2. Loomis, pp. 106-107, 112, 113, 127.
3. Knaggs, pp. 56, 59.
4. Brennan, pp. 1-5, 8, 83. Brennan identifies the man who is apparently Tomaki Mayazo as "Mr. Tanaki."

3. Out of Gas or Shot Down?

1. Brennan, *Witness to the Execution,* p. 93.
2. Ibid., *Witness,* p. 117.
3. Ibid., pp. 92-93; videotape.
4. Knaggs, p. 102.
5. Brennan, pp. 111, 117-118; videotape.
6. Ibid., p. 11.
7. Ibid., pp. 12-13.
8. Ibid., pp. 12-13.
9. Klaas, *Amelia Earhart Lives,* pp. 40-41.

197

4. Witness to Crash and Capture

1. Loomis, p. 89.
2. Knaggs, pp. 44-45, 48-50, 69, 122-127. The experiences of Loomis are found on pp. 44-45, 88-89, 105, 124. Those of Brennan are found on pp. 12, 93, 99-103.
3. Ibid., p. 43. Loomis also refers to Lijon: pp. 91-92, 105-106, 114, 121, 124.
4. Loomis, pp. 89, 92.
5. Ibid., pp. 87, 121.
6. Knaggs, p. 96.
7. Ibid., pp. 119-122
8. Loomis, pp. 90-92, 93, 95, 106, 121, 124. Also Knaggs, p. 50.
9. Loomis, pp. 88, 92, 106, 114.
10. Ibid., pp. 105-106.
11. Knaggs, pp. 43-49. Dominic is also mentioned by Brennan, p. 94.
12. Loomis, pp. 92, 114-115; Knaggs, pp. 43, 50, and chapter 10.

5. First Aid at Jaluit

1. Brennan, *Witness,* p. 104, and videotape: *Witness to the Execution, the Odyssey of Amelia Earhart.*
2. Loomis, pp. 107-113, 127.
3. Knaggs, pp. 52-56, 57, 59, 60.
4. Brennan, pp. 7, 82, 88, 103-107.
5. Prymak, *Trip to the Marshall Islands,* pp. IV-V.
6. Knaggs, pp. 55-59. Kabua Kabua is also mentioned by Loomis, pp. 93, 125.
7. Knaggs, p. 56. Kabua the Great is also mentioned by Loomis, pp. 84, 93.

6. Interrogation at Jaluit

1. Brennan, *Witness,* p. 101.
2. Loomis, pp. 84, 85, 86, 90. Amata Kabua is also mentioned by Knaggs (pp. 35, 41) and Brennan, (pp. 6-7, 73-76).
3. Ibid., p. 84.
4. Knaggs, pp. 35-36, 41.
5. Brennan, pp. 76-77, 97-98. Brennan calls de Brum "Oscar," not Tony.

7. Mysterious Missives

1. Knaggs, *Last Flight,* p. 72.
2. Goerner, p. 287.
3. Knaggs, pp. 72, 87.
4. Ibid., pp. 73-74, 100.
5. Knaggs, p. 99.
6. Brennan, p. 91.
7. Ibid., p. 2.

8. *Electra* to Emidj

1. Brennan, *Witness,* p. 89.
2. Goerner, p. 260-262.
3. Knaggs, p. 99.
4. Brennan, pp. 88-89; videotape.
5. Prymak, p. V.
6. Ibid., pp. 11-12.
7. Ibid., pp. 10-11.

9. American Veterans Speak Up

1. Goerner, *The Search for Amelia Earhart,* p. 278.
2. Ibid., pp.263-264, 265, 297, 305, ff.
3. Ibid., p. 188.
4. Ibid., pp. 277-278.
5. Ibid., pp. 278-279.
6. Ibid., p. 2.
7. Ibid., p. 4.
8. Ibid., pp. 172-173.
9. Ibid, pp. 185, 186-187, 232, 273.
10. Ibid., pp. 170-171.

10. Saipan Landing

1. Goerner, *Search,* p. 3.
2. Briand, *Daughter of the Sky,* pp. 212-214.
3. Goerner, pp. 1-6, 9, 42-43, 45, 48, 59, 284.
4. Ibid., p. 284.
5. Devine, pp. 109, 110, 118, A-15, A-17.

11. Interviews on Guam

1. Klaas, *Amelia Earhart Lives,* p. 86.
2. Ibid., pp. 80-81.
3. Ibid., pp. 74-81, 84, 93.
4. Ibid., pp. 80-81.
5. Ibid., pp. 75-76.
6. Ibid., p. 78.
7. Ibid., p. 78.
8. Ibid., pp. 78-79.
9. Ibid., pp. 84-87.
10. Ibid., pp. 88-89.
11. Ibid., pp. 112-113

12. Investigations Flourish on Saipan

1. Goerner, *Search,* pp. 49-50.
2. Ibid., pp. 2-3, 9-110, 39-42, 44.
3. Ibid., pp. 40-43, 47-48, 50.
4. Ibid., p. 47.
5. Ibid., pp. 47-48.
6. Ibid., p. 48.
7. Ibid., p. 48.
8. Ibid., p. 48.
9. Ibid., p. 48.
10. Ibid., pp. 2, 43, 44-45, 48, 51, 59, 97, 107, 238.
11. Devine, p. 71.
12. Goerner, pp. 49-50.
13. Ibid., pp. 49-50.
14. Ibid., pp. 50-51.
15. Ibid., p. 51.
16. Ibid., pp. 113-114.
17. Ibid., pp. 115-116.
18. Ibid., p. 116.
19. Klaas, pp. 117-118.
20. Ibid., p. 118.
21. Ibid., pp. 118-119.
22. Ibid., p. 119.
23. Ibid., p. 119.
24. Goerner, pp. 95-96.

25. Ibid., pp. 102-103.
26. Ibid., pp. 242-236.
27. Ibid., pp. 222f.
28. Devine, pp. 174-175.
29. Davidson, *Amelia Earhart Returns from Saipan,* pp. 166-173.

13. Hotel for Political Prisoners

1. Goerner, *Search,* p. 239.
2. Klaas, pp. 81-83.
3. Ibid., pp. 83-84.
4. Goerner, pp. 236, 239-240.
5. Brennan, pp. 115-116, also Klaas, p. 118.

14. The Ring and the Book

1. Knaggs, *Last Flight,* pp. 148-149.
2. Klaas, pp. 119-121. In the interview with Gervais, it was the sister who did the geography lesson, not Matilda.
3. Goerner, pp. 99-101. Goerner writes that in 1961, she was in her late thirties. This would have made her a teen-ager in 1937.
4. Davidson, pp. 93-95. Davidson states she was twenty-four in 1937. He also states that Matilda was married to a Japanese man named Shoda in 1937. After his death, she married a man named San Nicholas.
5. Knaggs, pp. 145-155. By 1977, Matilda's last name was Arriola. The interview reveals she was married in 1937.
6. Knaggs, pp. 165-167.

15. Cells No. 1 and 4

1. Knaggs, *Last Flight,* pp. 162-163.
2. Klaas, pp. 90-91.
3. Knaggs, pp. 156-164.
4. Goerner, p. 50.
5. Brennan, p. 124.

16. Their Deaths

1. Brennan, *Witness,* p. 127.
2. Goerner, pp. 99, 101-102.

3. Davidson, pp. 100, 103-104, 157-158.
4. Devine, pp. 152-153, 155, 156, 198.
5. Loomis, pp. 93-94.
6. Knaggs, pp. 172-173.
7. Ibid., pp. 173-176.
8. Brennan, pp. 125-129.

17. Their Burials

1. Devine, *Eyewitness: The Amelia Earhart Incident,* p. 62.
2. Ibid., pp. 60-62.
3. Klaas, pp. 89-90.
4. Ibid., pp. 89-90.
5. Goerner, pp. 310-311.
6. Ibid., p. 187.
7. Ibid., p. 102.
8. Ibid., p. 269.
9. Davidson, pp. 104, 158-166.
10. Ibid., pp. 181-183, 240-253.
11. Brennan, pp. 143-146.

18. Lost Legend

1. Long, *The Sound of Wings,* pp. 324, 377.
2. In articles he sent me and in a personal conversation.
3. *Life,* April 1992, pp. 68-74
4. *Weekly World,* April 28, 1992, pp. 46, 47
5. Andre, Henry Keyser, *Age of Heroes,* Hastings House. Information from book provided to me by members of the Amelia Earhart Society of Researchers.

Bibliography

BOOKS

Backus, Jean L. *Letters From Amelia.* Boston: Beacon Press, 1982.

Bendure, Glenda and Friary, Ned. *Micronesia: a Travel Survival Kit.* Berkeley, California, 1988.

Brennan, T.C. "Buddy." *Witness to the Execution.* Frederick, Colorado: Renaissance House, 1988.

Briand, Paul L., Jr. *Daughter of the Sky: The Story of Amelia Earhart.* New York: Duell, Sloan and Pearce, 1960.

Clark, David E., ed. *Islands of the South Pacific.* Menlo Park, California: Lane Publishing Co., 1986.

Cochran, Jacqueline, and Brinley, Maryann Bucknum. *Jackie Cochran.* New York: Bantam Books, 1987.

Davidson, Joe. *Amelia Earhart Returns from Saipan.* Canton, Ohio: Davidson Publishing Co., 1969.

De Leeuw, Adele. *The Story of Amelia Earhart.* New York: Grosset & Dunlop, 1955.

Devine, Thomas E. with Daley, Richard M. *Eyewitness: The Amelia Earhart Incident.* Frederick, Colorado: Renaissance House, 1987.

Devine, Thomas E. *The Involvement.* unpublished manuscript.

Donahue, James A. *The Earhart Disappearance:The British Connection.* Terre Haute, Indiana: Sunshine House, 1987.

Farrell, Don A. *Saipan.* Saipan, 1990.

Goerner, Fred. *The Search for Amelia Earhart.* Garden City, New York: Doubleday & Company, Inc., 1966.

Holden, Henry M., with Griffith, Captain Lori. *Ladybirds.* Mt. Freedom, New Jersey: Blackhawk Publishing Co., 1992.

Johnston, Richard W. *Follow Me: The Story of the Second Marine Division in World War II.* New York: Random House Press, 1948.

Kennedy, Arthur and Ridley, Jo Ann. *High Times: Keeping 'Em Flying.* Santa Barbara, California: Fithian Press, 1992.

Klaas, Joe. *Amelia Earhart Lives.* New York: McGraw Hill Book Company, 1970.

Knaggs, Oliver. *Amelia Earhart: Her Last Flight.* Capetown: Timmins, 1983.

Leder, Jane. *Amelia Earhart.* San Diego, California: Greenhaven Press, Inc., 1989.

Loomis, Vincent and Ethell, Jeffrey. *Amelia Earhart: The Final Story.* New York: Random House, 1985.

Lomax, Judy. *Women of the Air.* New York: Dodd, Mead and Co., 1987.

Lovell, Mary S, *The Sound of Wings.* New York: St. Martin's Press, 1989.

May, Charles Paul. *Women in Aeronautics.* New York: Thomas Nelson & Sons, 1962.

National Geographic *Atlas of the World.* Washington, D.C., 1970.

Pearce, Carol Ann. *Amelia Earhart*. New York: Facts on File Publications, 1988.

Randolph, Blyth. *Amelia Earhart*. New York: Franklin Watts, 1987.

Rich, Doris L. *Amelia Earhart*. Washington: Smithsonian Institution Press, 1989.

Shore, Nancy. *Amelia Earhart: Aviator*. New York: Chelsea House Publishers, 1987.

Sloate, Susan. *Amelia Earhart: Challenging the Skies*. New York: Fawcett Columbine, 1990.

Strippel, Dick. *Amelia Earhart: The Myth and the Reality*. New York Exposition Press, 1972.

Webster's New International Dictionary of the English Language, Second Edition, unabridged. Springfield, Massachussets: G.C. Merriam Company, Publishers, 1952.

ARTICLES, MAPS, MOTION PICTURES, A PLAY, PERIODICALS, AND TV PROGRAMS

A motion picture about the life of Amelia Earhart, made in the seventies.

A motion picture about the work of Richard Gillespie, made in 1992.

Flight for Freedom, a motion picture, 1942 or 1943.

Florida Today, April 9, 1992. pp. 1-2D.

Houston Post, March 17, 1992, p. A-4.

"In Search of Amelia Earhart," a television program originally produced in 1976, recently rebroadcast by the Arts and Entertainment channel.

Life, April, 1992, pp. 68-74. Gillespie, Richard, "The Mystery of Amelia Earhart."

Lost Electra (a play), by Bruce Rodgers.

Newsletters of the Amelia Earhart Society.

Pacific Sunday News, September 22, 1991, pp. 1, 3.

Plainfield (New Jersey) *Courier-News*, May 7, 1937, p. 1.

Tourist Map of Saipan, 1990. Saipan: Economic Service Counsel, Inc.

Tourist Map of Tinian, 1990. Saipan: Economic Service Counsel, Inc.

"Trip to the Marshall Islands." n.d., by Bill Prymak.

"Unsolved Mysteries" NBC-TV, November 7, 1990.

Weekly World, April 28, 1992. Denholm, Jill, "Amelia Earhart Found Alive."

Witness to the Execution: The Odyssey of Amelia Earhart: The Video, with T.C. "Buddy" Brennan.

Index

—A—

—C—

211

217

survival after crash, xvii, xviii, 35, 44, 52, 67, 92, 169
years mentioned by witnesses
  1937, xviii, 57, 69, 76, 87, 89, 92, 98, 100, 104, 112, 113, 114, 123, 126,
129, 139, 156, 171
    1938, 80, 129
    1944, 146

—O—

Ohasi, Maria, 122, 189
Okinawa, 96, 195
Okinawan woman, 155-156, 189
"Omnibus," 99

—P—

Pacific Island Monthly, 81
Pacific Ocean, xiii, xiv, xvii, xviii, 33, 36, 48, 51, 82, 90, 114, 136
Pacific Sunday News, 146
Palacious, Carlos, 128, 173, 174, 176, 177, 189
Palau, 69, 125, 196
Pangelinan, José, 115, 147, 158, 189
Parker, Alfred, 59, 190
Patton, Special Agent Joseph M., 99, 100, 103, 142, 144, 190
Penaluna, William, 96, 190
Phoenix Islands, 163, 196
Ponape, 125, 196
Pope, the, 120
Post, Wiley, xiv, 190
Prymak, Bill, xxi, 54, 58, 59, 68, 86, 87, 89, 190
Prymak, John, 68
Putnam, Miss Amelia Earhart, 82
Putnam, George, xvii, 190

—Q—

Queen of Mili, see Diklan, Queen Bosket, of Mili
Quintanilla, Guam Chief of Police, José, 101-102, 103-104, 113, 119, 120, 139, 190

—R—

Rafford, Paul L., Jr., xxi, 71, 190
Ratak Group, Marshall Islands, 82, 196
Reineck, Colonel (Ret.) Rollin C., xxi, 190
Renaissance House, 37
Reyes, Juan, 122, 190

About the Author

Donald Moyer Wilson's lifelong quest for knowledge and truth has culminated in this book, *Amelia Earhart: Lost Legend.*

Wilson was graduated with a major in Philosophy from Cornell University in 1948, (his studies were interrupted by a two year stint in the United States Marine Corps) a master of divinity degree from Union Theological Seminary, and a master of theology degree (with an emphasis on American church history) from Colgate Rochester Divinity School.

As part of the Second Marine Division, Wilson was stationed at Saipan, serving as rifleman and chaplain's assistant. Later he was with the division in Nagasaki and Sasebo, Japan after the end of World War II.

In 1951, he was ordained as a minister in the United Church of Christ, and married Vernajean Huyck. The couple have three children and three grandchildren.

Wilson served as a pastor of churches in Parkman, Ohio, and Flat Rock, Michigan, before moving to New York State. In 1962, he became associate pastor of the Irondequoit United Church of Christ, Rochester, New York. In 1969, he became pastor of the Henrietta, New York, United Church of Christ. Then in 1974, Wilson became a career agent for the Security Mutual Life Insurance Company of New York and earned the Chartered Life Underwriter and Chartered Financial Consultant designation. He has remained active in church service by serving as a supply preacher, interim pastor of the Perry Center United Church of Christ, pastor of the Riga United Church of Christ, and interim pastor of the Honeoye United Church of Christ.

In 1987, Wilson volunteered to teach various courses at the Rochester Institute of Technology's adult education program for

222

seniors known as The Athenaeum. His courses reflect his diverse areas of expertise: comparative religions; the nature of God; life after death, and the Amelia Earhart mystery.

With Vernajean, he has traveled to more than fifty countries. And he adds to his extraordinary range of talents and hobbies, sailing, hiking, canoeing, tennis, stamp collecting, astronomy, short-wave radio and music composition.

* * *

Author's note: The 1993 Amelia Earhart Symposium

After this book was written and while it was in production, I participated in the first symposium of the Amelia Earhart Society of Researchers in Morgan Hill, California, August 26-29, 1993. Among those with whom I visited who have been mentioned in this book were Bill Prymak, Paul L. Rafford, Jr., Albert Bresnik, Colonel (Ret.) Rollin C. Reineck, Jerome P. Steigmann, Joe Gervais, Joe Klaas, T. C. (Buddy) Brennan, Elgen Long and Jo Ann Ridley. I also had the opportunity to meet Louise Foudray, caretaker of the Amelia Earhart home in Atchison, Kansas, and Ann Holtgren Pellegreno, author of *World Flight: The Earhart Trail*, (Ames, Iowa: The Iowa State University Press, 1971) which tells how she flew around the world in a Lockheed 10A exactly thirty years after Amelia Earhart's venture and "completed" Earhart's flight as it was originally planned.

WORLD MAP

Route of Amelia Earhart's
Round the World Flight in 1937

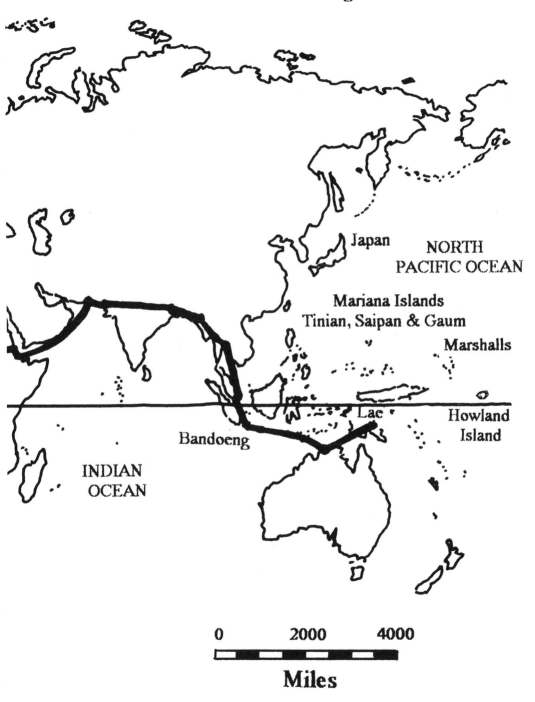

Japan

NORTH
PACIFIC OCEAN

Mariana Islands
Tinian, Saipan & Gaum

Marshalls

Lae

Howland
Island

Bandoeng

INDIAN
OCEAN

| 0 | 2000 | 4000 |

Miles